Persuasion Skills

BLACK BOOK

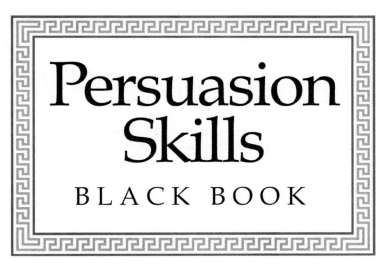

Persuasion Skills
BLACK BOOK

Practical NLP Language Patterns for
Getting The Response You Want

Rintu Basu

First Published In Great Britain 2009
by www.BookShaker.com

Typeset in Book Antiqua

Contents

Praise for The 'Black Book'

Rintu Basu believes my NLP trainings are so powerful and give you such an unfair advantage... they should almost be declared illegal. Obviously I won't debate him when he gives me such a compliment. And I doubt he'll debate me when I say his Persuasion Skills Black Book is excellent! He's crystallized some of the most powerful and potent NLP patterns you can humanly use to your advantage. The book is truly like enriched uranium, if you will, that can help you trigger a nuclear chain reaction of explosive benefits.

Kenrick E. Cleveland, world-famous creator of the Dark Side NLP Program, MAXPersuasion.com

Rintu's masterful use of language is only surpassed by his very clever way of making the complex very easy to understand. It is a real pleasure to see such a difficult subject broken down into simple, practical and usable chunks. Beginners and experts alike will find this book filled with useful information. The issue isn't the information but the results you get from using it and this book makes it easy to get results.

Romilla Ready, Lead Author, NLP for Dummies & NLP Workbook for Dummies

I wish [this book was] around when I was doing my NLP Training. I can't believe that twenty minutes reading your book put all my training in context so I can now easily use [technique edited]. I finally have the confidence to properly use hypnotic language in my presentations and with my teams and the results are showing already.

Richard, Sales Manager, Master NLP Practitioner

I have just read the [first pattern] of The Persuasion Skills Black Book and thought it was excellent. I am amazed at the insight required to write stuff like that. I will be honoured to have you as my 'NLP guru' in the future. Now I can't wait to go out and try this technique out on my patients and see the effects...

Dr Sri, NLP Newbie, Scotland 2007

The results are undeniable... the economy being what it is here in the U.S. and homeowners being very conservative where I live... our company has had a difficult couple of weeks. After employing [Rintu's] ideas I had a great week. Four sales and four happy customers last week.

Travis, Sales Professional, Home Improvement Industry

I started using the pattern in my calls on Friday afternoon and I closed more deals in that one afternoon than I would usually in 3 days, and Fridays are usually a slow day. I wasn't expecting instant results! It's great how you use examples and illustrations as well as sneaking all the patterns into your writing. Everyone would do better to understand persuasion skills this way, but I am glad they don't or I'd be out of a job.

Jamie, Sales Professional

Hi Rintu, I think your book needs to be required reading before you go on a practitioner course. I finished reading it toady and it puts all the language I learnt on my practitioner course into something I can use easily. I love the free downloads as well.

Jeff, UK

Rintu demonstrates by his writing that he walks what he talks... what he demonstrates is actually his deep understanding and mastery of the mind rather than the use of language alone... I feel compelled to read on and on, not, because of the hypnotic language pattern but because it is a real pleasure to keep reading and learning from Rintu. I have actually read a dozen books on NLP (in English or Chinese) and none of them (I mean on the topic of hypnotic language pattern) comes near to this. The first 24 pages already worth the price of the whole book.

Liu Yui Kai, Physician, Hong Kong

Hi Rintu, I bought your book to read over Christmas and can't say I have laughed so much at a book for a long time.

I have been a Master Prac of NLP for five years so many of the patterns and ideas I have seen before. What got me was the clever (and sometimes not so clever ways you covertly demonstrate all of the patterns several times before telling anyone what you are doing.

I went through the book three or four times just catching all the language you were using. I have to say I learnt a lot just from watching how you keep setting up each pattern before teaching it.

Thanks for a great read that has obviously been very skilfully put together.

Carole, Master Practitioner, UK

Hey Rintu, Just need to tell you about an incredible result yesterday. I bought your book last week and was doing the exercise about using the patterns on myself. There is a girl at work that used to frighten me a lot. I was using the patterns on myself to stop me acting like an idiot every time she came anywhere near me.

I went back to work yesterday and the first thing that happened was she came up and asked about my holidays. In the next few minutes I used hundreds of things from the book and asked her out on a date. I'm now taking her out for a meal on Friday night. The old me couldn't have done that. Thanks, the book is brilliant.

Gareth, UK

Hi Rintu, Love the book. I read it in two days, but the reason I am really writing is I had my end of year review and used your techniques. I have had a few days illness this year and knew it would be brought up in my review. So I used your pattern and said to my manager "The issue is not my illness but the work I do when I'm here. Let's talk about my achievements." My manager agreed and I got a better grade than I was expecting. I didn't expect it to be this easy.

Cathy, USA

Acknowledgements

I have been blessed with a lot of good friends and colleagues that have helped me to get this book published. Some have gone so far beyond the call of duty that they deserve special mention.

My thanks go to my parents for their unwavering support even when they didn't understand the strange directions their son's life went in.

To Dave for the genius technical wizardry and insight that made the website and the original course possible. But even more so for walking the road with me and being the long-suffering test subject for all my patterns. Dave, I hope the nightmares stop soon.

To Romilla for the support, companionship and those long discussions about life the universe and everything, as well as giving me the inspiration to write a book of my own. Long may the lunches continue.

To Peter for bailing me out when I was fresh out of ideas with my back against the wall and nowhere to run. This project would have been dead in the water without your timely assistance. If there had been anyone sensible to talk to on that course I may never have found you.

To Debbie and her team who made this project possible despite my inexperienced stumbling into the book world.

And finally to those mentors, teachers and students throughout my life that have taught me enough to occasionally say something worth listening to.

FREE Platinum Black Book Persuasion Programme

Dear Reader,

I am so keen to ensure that you get results from my book that I would like to invite you to join the Platinum Black Book Training Programme completely free of charge.

This free programme will be delivered by email and will contain lessons and downloads to further build on what you will learn in this book.

Included in this complimentary programme are audio and video presentations and a slew of new patterns.

So, if you haven't already, be sure to read this book straight away, practice the techniques, enrol on the course and find yourself getting more of what you want.

You can sign up right now at...

www.theNLPcompany.com/bonus18683

Best Wishes

Rintu

Foreword

I wish I had had a book like this when I was learning NLP!

I was really thrilled and honoured when Rintu asked me to write the foreword to 'The Persuasion Skills Black Book' because it's time for him to share his phenomenal knowledge of NLP.

This book contains a **lot of material** and might have been quite overwhelming for some except... for the way that the lessons have been broken up into very manageable and easy to learn chunks.

Not only does Rintu give a mass of hints and tips on how and what to practice, he plays the part of a virtual coach, keeping the need to practice in your awareness.

You know how it is, when one becomes so familiar with something that aspects of it become second nature to you? There are some things in NLP that I do unconsciously and in going through 'The Persuasion Skills Black Book', I realised there are some really powerful language techniques that I'd forgotten about and have made a conscious effort to build into my repertoire of persuasive linguistics.

Rintu and I started our NLP training, what seems, a lifetime ago and I was amazed at how fearlessly he 'played' with what we were learning and as a result displayed a confidence and expertise far beyond someone starting on their NLP journey.

I hope you enjoy this terrific book as much as I have. I am sure you will find it is a really useful resource.

Oh! And... even when you think you've learned it all, keep coming back to it and challenge yourself to build on what you've learned and consigned to your unconscious and like me, you'll be bound to find new and innovative ways to broaden your expertise.

Romilla Ready
Lead Author of *Neuro-linguistic Programming for Dummies®*
(a top selling for Dummies® book which has been translated into 8 languages)
and *Neuro-linguistic Programming Workbook for Dummies®*

Preface

The Learning of Hypnotic Language Patterns is Easy

Welcome to your quick start guide to NLP language patterns.

It is great to have you here, reading these words and wanting to ramp up your persuasion skills. I can get very excited when I think about the results you are likely to create using this material. If you spend a few minutes thinking about where, when and what results you are looking for I would guess you can get excited as well.

I am not going to promise you any results... I am going to promise you some of the best information on NLP, psychological and hypnotic persuasion language. I am going to promise you lots of examples to give you ideas how you can use this material. I am going to promise you many conscious and unconscious ways of developing and learning these skills. If you make a commitment to getting the results you want then I know this material will help.

As the interest in NLP, covert persuasion, conversational hypnosis and persuasive language patterns grows there seems to be more confusion and less quality information both in books and on the internet.

The learning of hypnotic language patterns is easy when approached well. This book is designed to be a quick start guide that will allow you some incredible quick wins whilst building you a few solid foundations to spring from. It is not meant to be an academic piece of work, nor is it meant to be read and put on a shelf. Since you have made the commitment to buy this book, make a commitment to yourself to go out and play with the material.

It is important to note that this is not a complete NLP language course. Whilst it does contain much that NLP Practitioners and Master Practitioners don't know about Persuasive Language it is not a complete body of work.

This book was designed specifically for quick wins with short snappy usable and practical patterns you can start using anywhere.

This book was originally designed as a course to be read in bi-weekly chunks via email. I have kept the same format with some editing to make the material more appropriate for a book. There is a lot of demonstration of patterns throughout this book. For the most part I have deliberately kept the language with my normal (bad) sense of grammar and as I would speak.

Often introducing the patterns takes longer than the pattern itself. This is because right through the book you will find me demonstrating the patterns. Look out for this and see if you can catch the patterns before I explain them to you.

Values, Ethics & Manipulation
You are Responsible for Your Results

A quick word about values, ethics and manipulation. I am not the NLP Thought Police and nor will I allow myself to be set up for this. What you do with these patterns is for you to decide. I will urge you to have good intent, leave people in a better place than you found them in and always work towards win/win situations. I don't say this through any altruistic, tree hugging or saintly attitude. It simply makes sense. If you con, trick and force people against their will you will be caught out eventually. As a result you will lose credibility, trust and friendship.

Being honest, direct and open in your dealings with people gives you a huge amount of personal power. You will gain more business, more friends and a reputation that attracts people to you. And even better - they will want to do the things you want them to and give their effort freely because you are open about how they also benefit. Trust me, I've tried it both ways and the second works so much better, is more long lasting and makes me feel good to boot.

Anyway, back to the real point, we will talk about each pattern in isolation, why it works, where you would use it,

1

how you can practice it and finally other contexts and applications. I will show you how to set each pattern up to deliver results. We will talk about the results you can expect and how you follow through for different contexts.

How To Use This Book

Learning Patterns is Supposed to be Fun

We will look at patterns designed to shift resistance, focus people on your results, embed hypnotic commands and generally move people in the direction you want them to go in.

You will find that I am deliberately finding ways of using these patterns in my introduction to them. Sometimes even a couple of chapters ahead. I have also deliberately tried to keep my language colloquial and as I would speak. This is to give you examples of how these patterns work in the spoken form. This is not always easy, as the emphasis and pauses are not always the same as the written form. If you find a few passages that don't read right just say them out loud a few times changing the emphasis on particular words. You will find out a whole lot about embedded commands and how you can use them through this method.

Every one of the patterns you will learn are designed to be quick, easy to use and can be integrated into normal language very easily. But you do need some practice and thought to be given to make this exceptionally powerful for you. So it is important to discuss how you will practice these patterns in the real world.

Since you have the complete book in your hands you can obviously flick through in any order, skip lessons and generally use it how you like. I would suggest that whilst it is easy to pick up the pace you will get the best if you go through it in order and try each section out as it comes up.

The sections all build on each other so it is designed to be read and used in order. Whilst it is great to read ahead I would suggest that you learn each pattern, go and use it and then move on to the next.

With regard to practice it is important to note that there is a difference between thinking things through and saying things out loud. Saying a thing out loud is different if you are on your own or practicing with someone. Just to spell it out completely:

1. Figure out the pattern in your head.
2. Read through the lesson again looking for the covert examples.
3. Check the examples and applications at the end of the 'theory'.
4. Write out some examples that you can use.
5. Say them out loud to yourself.
6. Find a study buddy and role play a conversation in a safe environment.
7. Go and use the pattern live with people in as many situations you can.

8. Suddenly find yourself using the patterns where it matters.

If you think it is unnecessary to learn any of the patterns then just skip to the next. Remember the main point is to over-practice to the point where these patterns are natural, instinctive and you use them without thinking.

There is a difference between using and practicing. Going into the most important meeting of your life is not the time to practice new patterns; it's the time to use what you have already learned and are comfortable with.

All of your growth, learning and development is outside of your normal routines. This means you have to try new things to grow. The follow on is that you will not be perfect and get things right straight away. I would suggest that you develop the opportunity to laugh at yourself, get found out using patterns and enjoy getting it wrong as much as making it work. Trust me; you will develop faster this way. So with this in mind find innocent members of the public and bury them under a barrage of language patterns.

Ten Minutes Daily Practice

Ten Minutes a Day Is Worth Much More
Than 70 Minutes a Week

One thing that we are looking to do is to set up some consistent routines and habitual patterns. The easiest way of doing this is to set aside some time daily for practicing and developing your persuasion skills.

Realistically if I asked you for half an hour or an hour a day I am unlikely to get it over the long-term. But there is no excuse for not finding ten minutes. Everyone can find that in a day even if it is at the end of an exhausting, bad day when you are not in the mood… you can still find ten minutes for practice.

You also learn better and faster in regular quick chunks that are smaller than your attention span. Ten minutes daily is worth much more than 70 minutes once a week.

Feel free to do as many ten minute chunks every day as you please, so long as you do ten minutes at a time and you do at least one ten minute chunk every day.

The ten minute chunks can be anything from the list on page 4 so long as you spend most of your time with step 7 - using the pattern live with people in as many situations you can.

Key Points

- Ten minutes a day is worth far more than 70 minutes per week.

- Practice is different from using, so practice until you just instinctively use it.

- Have fun, be prepared to laugh and fall over as you learn.

Changing The Direction of A Person's Thoughts

The Redefine – Your First Persuasion Pattern

L et us move into our first pattern. In NLP jargon terms this is called a 'Redefine'. But the issue isn't what it is called, but how do you use it… so let us talk about that.

The pattern is used to move the conversation from one subject to another. Again the issue is not about what it does, it's actually about the results it creates. So, the results you can get from this are to move the listener from their current thoughts to a new direction.

I am guessing now the issue is not the results, but when am I actually going to give you the pattern. The reason I am holding off for a moment is not because I am holding anything back, just simply because I want you to understand how easy and powerfully you can change the direction of a person's thoughts with a pattern like this. With this pattern you can start with any subject and move to any other subject. The real issue is not about this pattern but why we are not talking about the socio-economic policies of

Thailand... what do you think about how the economy in Thailand changes their social landscape?

I understand that you now really want to know the pattern, but the real issue is fully understanding the wide range of applications for a pattern like this... so let us think about where you would want to use this sort of pattern first.

- The most obvious would be when you are arguing with someone and they are stuck on one point that you want to move away from.

- How about in sales when your customer has come up with an objection and you want to talk about the benefits of your product.

- As a trainer, a group might be starting to discuss issues that are not relevant to the topic in hand and you want to bring them back to the point of the lesson.

- Perhaps in a flirting situation where your flirting partner is talking about how the rest of the office will gossip and you want to talk about dinner arrangements.

Does that give you some idea of the range of applications for this pattern? The issue is not the amount of applications I can think of, it is all about how many applications you can come up with. So just for a few moments think about times and situations where you want to change the direction or flow of a conversation.

Now that you have done that here is the pattern:

"The issue isn't (x), it's (y) and that means…"

x is the thing you are talking about and y the thing you want to talk about.

The issue isn't about trying to understand the formula, it's simply about just using it and that makes it very easy to use… doesn't it?

The beauty of a pattern like this is that you don't need to think about it and you can move the conversation into anything you want, particularly if you ask questions based on the new subject. Here is an example.

Let's say I am in a group of business people at a networking event and they are all complaining about problems in their companies and I want to talk to them about communications courses.

I might say something like, *"The issue isn't about the result you are getting, but how your people are not solving these problems themselves… what is it about your staff that means they are not solving these problems for themselves?"*

This might get the group talking about the problems with their staff and after a while I might interject with, *"The fact that they are not taking the initiative is a problem, but the bigger issue is how well the managers are communicating the vision to their staff… how good are your managers at this?"*

Maybe now they are discussing the communications skills of their managers and I am going in with, "The issue is not about the fact they are not doing a good job but how well you are supporting them to get better at it... what communications training have they done?"

Now they might be talking about how little training they have done, but also how expensive training is and that they can't afford it. I might start in with, "The issue is not the expense of training, but how much poor performance is costing you... if I can show you a way of getting a return of investment from your training budget would you be interested in talking about how you can do that?"

Okay, I have a whole range of tools, as you will have by the end of this book so I probably would have used a variety of methods to get to this point with the group, but you could do it with just this one pattern. It's that effective. In fact, if you were brave enough you could have done it in one move...

The 'One Move' Example

Let's go back to the start of the conversation and they are discussing their business problems. You could just launch in with:

> *"The issue isn't the problems in your business but how much support you are giving your people to improve, how good a result would you get if you invested in communications skills training for all of them?"*

I prefer leading people in small steps rather than just plunging for the jugular, but the issue here is to just notice that you can take one big step to move in a different direction.

So long as you have some rapport and ask a question you will have moved the conversation to where you want it to go.

Later in the book we will discuss how to build rapport, non-verbally, tonally and linguistically. Other ideas you might like to explore include borrowing rapport from others (great to do if a very popular speaker has been speaking just before your spot), and binding rapport so that people keep thinking about you and feel good whenever they see you.

Applications of 'Redefine Patterns'

Now you know how to change the direction of thoughts how are you going to use it?

Before we look at some more applications, just read the beginning of this chapter again and notice how many times I cycle you through the pattern. Now let us look at some more applications.

ARGUMENTS

The issue is not (their point), but (my point), and then ask a question to get them to focus on your point. For example:

> *"The issue is not about western oil interests in the Middle East but about the bombing of innocent victims from both sides, what measures can we start putting into place to ensure a move towards peace?"*

Or if you are feeling particularly nasty:

"The issue is not about the point you are doggedly holding on to but your insecurity in having to hold a fixed position, what are you going to do to increase your self-esteem?"

FLIRTING

"The issue is not how much we are going to be talked about in the office, but are we going to give them something to really talk about, what would you say if we were to take the afternoon off, go back to my place and…"

SALES

"The issue is not about the expense of the Beginner's Guide to Advanced Persuasion Patterns but about how for less than the price of a daily cup of coffee and the time it takes to drink it I can show you how you can powerfully enhance your persuasion skills?"

HOW ABOUT THE MOST EXTREME
SALES EXAMPLE I CAN THINK OF…

"You make a valid point in that you have no use for the product at all, but the real issue is about how much fun you have writing big cheques, tell me how big that cheque has to be in order to split your sides with laughter as you hand it over to me?"

I don't really expect that one to work… but it might be worth a go sometime.

I can carry on coming up with examples all afternoon, but the point has been made and you are already getting the idea of how to use this pattern, aren't you?

So for a few minutes think about where, when and how you will use this pattern.

Practicing Patterns

Take the opportunity to think up the phrases and practice saying them out loud. To get to be spontaneous with these patterns is to spend some time thinking about how you would use them and then spend some time saying the patterns out loud so your mouth gets used to saying them.

We will talk more about practicing and combining patterns as we go through the book, but for the moment, read through this lesson again and notice how many times and variations of this pattern I have used, get use to saying it and then go and unleash this pattern on some unsuspecting member of the public.

Next I will show you a pattern that will allow you to attach conditions to anything that is said. You might think that a little ambitious, I would agree with you and just imagine if it were possible... could you have fun with the idea?

Go play, have fun, and remember the issue is not about having to learn complex patterns but to take a simple idea and just use it to get results. Just ten minutes a day firing patterns at poor unsuspecting members of the public.

Are You Committed To Learning Persuasion Skills?

I hope you have had the time to go through the first pattern and are already putting it into action. You are only just past the first pattern and I am already badgering you about how much you are doing with it.

Here is my thinking… I know this is a really powerful book. I also know it is more powerful than the majority of courses, written, audio visual or face to face that you can get. There are two reasons I am giving you this material. Firstly, as a trainer, I love seeing people get results. Secondly, as a businessman, I need to make money. Neither of these things will happen unless you take action and do things with this material.

Some take the approach of the info junkie that just has to hoard knowledge. But consider this; knowledge only brings power if you do something with it. You could make a commitment to yourself to grow, develop and learn new skills and if you did then you will find that what you learn in this book will give you a huge boost to your success.

You have already made a commitment by purchasing this book, so taking the final step of using the material is easy. I will do as much as I can to help. That includes the free video presentation in the bonus course that comes with this book, the additional material on the Facebook Fan page at *www.fbook.me/persuasion* and, of course, live examples of all the patterns, tactics and ideas that I discuss with you on my blog.

What are you prepared to commit to seriously enhancing your persuasion skills? It will take a little more than just reading this book.

If you are prepared to learn, grow and develop then the issue is not the quality of the content but the commitment you make in learning to use it.

If you are following this argument so far, you made a commitment of purchasing this book, you made a commitment to read this far I am asking you for a commitment to thinking about the results that you can get by developing your persuasion skills further. Since you have read this far I am assuming that there are results that you want. Balance the results that you are after against spending ten minutes daily for the next few weeks to enhance your skills.

And to take this one step further, the issue is not learning to use it but in creating results from using it. This means you need to practice and I am back at my original question, "Are you committed to learning persuasion skills?"

More Examples & Illustrations of Redefine Patterns

The only real issue is how are you going to use this pattern?

Next you will learn a pattern you can use to make a really big impact when you deliver the redefine pattern. I want you to be ready for it. So if you have not yet been going round redefining everyone's thoughts then get going because the second lesson is going to add something special to the mix.

Here are a few more examples.

There have been a couple of really good results from the redefine pattern we discussed:

1. One guy going for a job that he clearly didn't have the experience for when asked said, *"The issue is not my lack of experience but whether I can get results for you, let me explain how I am going to get you better results than any of your experienced employees."* He got the job.

2. A bargain hunter said, *"The issue is not how good the car is but what kind of discount you are going to give me so you can make the sale, if you give me another 10% I'll take the car right now."* He got the discount.

3. And a failure... but top marks for the attempt, *"The issue is not us going out together but whether we have sex, so how about us going back to my place now?"* Didn't quite work, but great attempt.

Send in examples, testimonials and field reports to *www.thenlpcompany.com/techniques/contact-us* Remember there will be prizes, including discounts on courses and free copies of the updated versions of this book if I use your examples.

Here is a pattern that I think is brilliant that has come from an entry to a competition I ran for free places on *Advanced Persuasion Patterns*, a download persuasion skills course:

"The issue isn't if I won the free course/book, but how are you going to choose the other winner?"

Agreement Frames

How to Agree with Everything and Still Get Your Own Way

H ere's an explosively brilliant pattern for you. The
pattern sets up an agreement frame even when
there is none.

Why do this?

Well without losing your integrity you can use this
pattern to lower someone's defences and get them to
really listen to you. In short you can use this to bypass a
person's conscious and unconscious defences and deal
directly with what matters... i.e. listening to you.

And if you use this with the redefine pattern you can
bypass all conscious thoughts and totally redefine the
direction of the conversation. Trust me, many Master
Practitioners and Practitioners don't have these patterns.

Gaining Agreement & Attaching
Conditions So They Can't Say No

This pattern will allow you to attach conditions to
whatever has been said before. Even to the point where
you can attach the completely opposite view.

This pattern allows you to bypass the original comment
and move the conversation on to agreement with you. I

will even show you a super pattern combining the last two lessons that is designed to completely move the conversation to exactly where you want it.

Agreement Frames

We are about to talk about an amazingly powerful pattern called an agreement frame. I agree that we should get on with the pattern and would add that a little discussion about how you say things will make a huge difference to the pattern working or not. So we are going to spend a few minutes discussing that first.

The failure or success of these patterns depends on your rapport with the subject and how you say the pattern. I'm not going to say much about this here because there is a section covering the basics coming up.

Are you ready for the pattern? I agree and that is why we are going to talk about pitch, pace and tone first. Most people speak too fast for real influencing power. To really reach the core of a person's being you need to speak in slow, deep tones. This is not about saying one word and having a pause before the next word... it is about slowing down how you say the words altogether. Here is an exercise you will benefit from.

A Simple Practice Routine

Every morning in the bathroom spend a few minutes talking to yourself in the mirror. Practice these patterns out loud in a slow, deep voice. Really exaggerate, drawing the words out using your best Barry White voice.

If you over compensate when you practice the chances are you will get it about right when you do this for real. Trust me, this will make the difference, great patterns delivered well get results. If you agree you deserve the best results in the fastest time I would suggest that you commit to spending a few minutes a day practicing. Better still you can take this as part of your ten minutes a day.

Agreement Frames Again

Anyway, let's move into the pattern, the agreement frame. This pattern works on the basis that people like to be agreed with. Often to the point that the words "I agree" are enough for them. Think about this for a moment. If I said I disagreed with you it would feel worse than if I said I agreed. In fact what I am agreeing or not agreeing with is almost irrelevant at this point. I agree, you might find this a little strange and what I would suggest you do is a little experiment. For the rest of the day in every conversation just randomly say "I agree" or "I disagree" with whatever statements are made by people.

My guess is that they will hallucinate what they think you are disagreeing/agreeing with and react accordingly. Whichever way you look at it they will react well to agreement and badly to disagreement without you ever qualifying what you are agreeing with.

We can use this quirky little feature to move conversations to where we want them to go. So here is the pattern:

"I agree... and would add..."

Here is an example:

> *"I agree the course is expensive and that is why it is packed full of so much useful information."*

Or with my super pattern:

> *"I agree the course is expensive and would add the issue is not the expense, but how much money you will make from going on the course."*

Agree to Everything?

Are you already noticing how powerful this pattern can be? Often at this point people start to say but what if I don't agree with the previous statement... I can't just say I agree for the sake of it. I agree with you and would also say you can just agree with the part of the statement that you do agree with. In the worst possible case you can always agree with the fact that the person made the statement. Let me give you an example.

Let's just say someone has said something I completely dislike and I really want to put them down, I might say something like:

> *"I agree you said that and would add only a complete idiot would have said it."*

But why not just tell the guy that he is an idiot I hear you cry. Well, I really want him to get the idea that he is an idiot. If I just started attacking him or saying I disagree he would not be listening to me, he would be preparing to defend himself. By starting with an agreement frame his defences are down and he is getting prepared to hear all the great things I am going to say about how right he is. That means he will be listening to the harsh words that follow.

Most of the time I am not operating from such an extreme position. Usually I am looking to make a point that is different and not normally trying to create a fight. In those sorts of circumstances the phrase might come out like:

"I agree that you said that and I would add that there is a different way of looking at it that would get you a better result."

Or something similar. Now let me talk about the one thing you have to get right to make this pattern work. That is the word "and". Compare the two phrases below:

1. *"I agree <u>but</u> what I would add is…"*

2. *"I agree <u>and</u> what I would add is…"*

Can you see the first doesn't work and the second has much greater impact? If you don't see it, go find a few people to play with, try both phrases and just notice their reactions to both statements.

We will come back to how you can use "and", "but" and others words to create deletions and additions to the way someone thinks. But for the moment I want to share some other ways of delivering an agreement phrase.

Variations on a Theme

One of the ways I use this pattern is to create a little confusion that creates more anticipation and keeps you listening even harder to my response.

Consider what happens if you make a statement and I respond with, "I almost agree with you and…"

You are left with what bits did he agree with and you are going to listen more intently to me to find out what bits I agree with. Here are some other versions of this opening. All of which I use and most of the time you can simply decide on your favourites and just practice them. Each of these create different effects, but so long as you have the basic pattern, the rest can follow:

"I don't completely agree with all of what you said and…"

"I agree with almost all of that and…"

"Can I check that I agree and add…"

"I totally agree you said (x) and…"

I am sure you can think of a few more and that means we can move on to the second half of the phrase.

Second Half of The Phrase

My two versions of what I put after the "and" are:

"…and what I would add is…"

"…and that means…"

If you have got this then let us look at a few examples.

SALES

"I agree it is expensive and that means you will get a better quality product."

TRAINING

"I agree you don't understand yet and that means you are still processing the information, come back this afternoon if you have not thought it through by then."

DELEGATING

"I totally agree that you appear overworked and that is why I am suggesting we set some time aside to go through your priorities so you can do the things that are important."

BEING DELEGATED TO

"I agree this new task is important and that means it should be given to someone who has the spare capacity to deal with it."

RELATIONSHIPS

"I agree I don't say 'I love you' and here are all the ways I demonstrate my love for you…"

If you think of a few applications you will suddenly realise how powerful this pattern is and that means you will be ready for the next chapter where you will discover some really clever ways of deleting, adding and joining random elements to a conversation to move people to your outcomes.

In the meantime practice this pattern out loud a few times and then find some innocent victims to agree with.

Practicing Being Persuasive
More Ideas On How To Practice Your New Found Skills

Here is just a quick note about how to practice persuasion patterns. I thought it would be a good idea to share my thoughts before the next lesson as what is coming up is one of the most powerful patterns you can get. Obviously this does not include the chapter on how to build anticipation loops, but we will get to that one a little later.

It is a pattern that allows you to slip assumptions into your language that will never be challenged. Consider the benefits of being able to take an idea that you want someone to have and to be able make them think that they have always had the thought. Now the patterns for this chapter are almost that powerful, and the only reason I say 'almost' is because in certain circumstances you need to think them out properly to make them work.

So, about practice… firstly let me suggest that when the stakes are high, the emotions are flowing and you really need a result, this would not be a good time to practice. Why not? Because the result is more important than the practice. Your aim should be to practice when it is relaxed, fun and the results don't matter. And practice so much that when it does matter everything happens instinctively.

So, repetition helps, being relaxed helps, having fun helps. Have you heard any of this before? And if it seems familiar just read back over some of this material and consider why it has been written the way it has. Anyway, here are a few ideas for you.

When you read the chapter have a context or situation in mind. As soon as you have finished think about how you will use the information. The more vividly you can imagine yourself using the information the better. Write out a few patterns that you can use and practice them out loud with yourself.

Find simple situations where you can just blurt out the patterns with someone else where it doesn't matter. Spend a few minutes every day thinking about where you could have used the pattern and forgot, or didn't realise at the time. Replay these situations and imagine yourself using the patterns. This is setting your unconscious mind in the right direction.

Find places, situations and people where the result is not important and just go for it. When I learn new patterns I write three or four of them out the night before based on what I think will happen the next day. I then make a commitment to myself to say the patterns to someone what ever else happens during the day. I get myself some very strange looks, some very odd situations and often some great results that you could never have predicted. But the whole point is I am practicing these patterns so when I need them they happen automatically.

Ideas From How Others Are Using These Patterns

Marcus sent me an email with an example of what he has done with it.

> A more powerful way of using the extreme one-move use of the procedure is to make an implicit suggestion. I have actually seen the extreme example you gave, in action. I met an old friend in a shop where he was looking at TVs.
>
> He prides himself on being able to spend more than anyone else. He asked me about the technical merits of plasma versus LCD TVs and I suggested plasmas were sharper but they had a shorter life expectancy, but of course they were outrageously more expensive, especially in the larger sizes. I could see the moment when his thinking shifted from the technical facts to the cost.
>
> He left the shop with the biggest plasma TV they had, and made sure I knew it was their most expensive TV. I think that was an example of implying the issue wasn't the technicalities, but the cost. It probably helped that I knew his triggers and his likely response... and he's still a friend.

This is a brilliant example of using the redefine pattern because Marcus has adapted it to set off his friend's hot buttons.

Briefly let me demonstrate how you might use this sort of thing. Let's just take a sales context where I am selling a product and I have uncovered several pieces of information about the prospect:

- She is self-referential i.e. *she* wants to make the decision, not get pushed into it.
- She is motivated by return on investment.
- She does not like taking risks.

Obviously we would be in conversation and I would probably use different patterns, many of which are in this book, but restricting things to the first two patterns:

"I agree it seems like a risk and I would add that the issue is not the risk but the return of investment you will make, but only you can decide that. What would you have to realise about the product to make your decision today?"

The last question is outside the scope of the first two lessons so come back to this example once you have read the chapter on Questioning.

A brilliant and insightful email again from Marcus has given me the opportunity to explain a very rapid trance induction technique. Here is the email.

I agree that this is a powerful pattern, and I agree that it can be used to deflect objections, and I agree that it can be made even more powerful in the next lesson; so I know you believe it can be used in the form of a 3-stage "yes step" induction.

Customer in garage:

I agree the colour is right, and I certainly agree it's well equipped, and I agree it performs better than the old model, so I know you'll want to help me with the price.

You'd use words other than "I agree" all the time though, to keep the flow of the language going.

The interesting question is whether that third "I agree" can be "I almost agree" without disrupting the pattern. Maybe it will make the pattern more effective. I've used that, but never noted the results.

Thanks for the Lesson.

Sales Technique: Building 'Yes Sets'

I almost agree with what Marcus is saying here and would add the following. Building yes sets is an old style sales technique that has great applications although I use them slightly differently. The standard pattern is just about getting your prospect to stay saying yes so when you ask them if they are ready to hand over the cheque it is easy for them to continue saying yes.

NLP Technique: 'Hypnotic Pacing & Leading'

This is the root of hypnotic pacing and leading techniques. Essentially, by making sensory based statements that are absolutely and verifiably true, your unconscious mind has to agree with what is being said. You then add a statement that is not verifiable but you want to be true for your client and it becomes easy to follow along.

Here is an example:

> *"As you are holding this book, reading these words you are going further into a trance."*

The first two statements are true, the third may or may not be, but it is easy to follow along. Having read this and having got an understanding of the concept, you are eager to learn more. And that is a good thing because you will find more about hypnotic pacing and leading later.

What I would like to lead on to now is a very powerful NLP technique called a pattern interrupt.

Hypnotic Technique: 'NLP Pattern Interrupt'

The basic idea is that people like to follow a coherent pattern of ideas, thoughts or events. When this pattern is broken an element of confusion is created and that can lead to instantaneous hypnotic trance.

Some of you will have seen or heard of handshake inductions used by some NLP Trainers, especially Richard Bandler. This works from the same principles. So let us talk a little more about how pattern interrupts might work in a persuasion setting instead. It is easier to explain through example so let me give you an example of a pattern interrupt and then deconstruct it.

'Pattern Interrupt' Example

For a variety of reasons that are not relevant here, three rather violent men in a pub were once accosting me. As they approached offering me a violent outcome I raised my voice and said something like, *"Sh*t, I forgot the kittens!"* The lead guy stopped, looked at me and started saying something when I interrupted, still in a loud voice but gradually calming down, with something like, *"If I had the kittens, you would want to stroke them wouldn't you!"*

Let us pause for a moment here and deconstruct what is going on. Firstly, the guys coming towards me have already planned out in their heads how this action is supposed to play out. I interrupted the pattern with a completely off the wall comment which stopped them dead in their tracks because it made no sense. Before they could put some pattern of their normality back into it I have followed up with a direct command about what they would do if the kittens were there (hence the exclamation rather than a question mark. This is an 'embedded command' for those of you that like the jargon.)

From a non verbal perspective I have paced their style and speech initially (I built rapport) and after interrupting the pattern gradually brought my tone, voice and manner down to something non aggressive (lead them).

Within a few minutes I had all three holding and stroking imaginary kittens tickling them under the chin and scratching them behind the ears.

What Marcus has hit upon in his email is an even more sneaky persuasion strategy. And that is to install the pattern in the first place and then break it. Then by breaking it you can send them into an instantaneous trance state where you may well be able to load in a few embedded commands. I should leave you with some ideas of the benefits you could get from learning that one pattern, but I guess you are already thinking of many of your own.

Changing Perceptions

Below is an email from Jan who is getting some great results already from the first two patterns ('redefine' and 'agreement frames'). I have included the email because there are a couple of really good points that are worth bringing up about persuasion and influence that will help you boost your results.

I'll let you read the email first.

Hi Rintu,

I appreciate the examples provided in the first two lessons and the practical application examples you provide.

I manage an operation where I employ between 11 to 14 individuals at a time.

All of these people come from different ethnic backgrounds, with different upbringings and all of them have very different core values and beliefs. I used the "I agree" statement today in my interactions with different employees and in many instances; it was to sort perceptions of the company's approach to profitability or to delegate. When I used the "I agree" statement in sorting perceptions it validated what I always believed - that two parallel truths can co-exist.

I used the "I agree" statement in the exact example used in lesson two - I was delegating a new task to an employee who had a concern with time constraints and I was able to say, "I agree and this is why time management will be crucial, lets take some time to review how this can be accomplished without impacting your time."

You have me fired up and I am excited to learn more.

Thank you.

Jan

Perceptual Positions & The Nature of Reality

Jan's comment about "two parallel truths" is spot on and can really help your persuasion skills. The only perspective you really have on a situation is your own. And the one you need to understand for great persuasion skills is your subject's.

For example, when I was a junior trainer in a large organization there was a need for me to move in to an evaluation team. Anyone that knows me will also know I am hopeless at detail, numbers and spreadsheets because I hate it (for you NLPers out there, yes I can change it... and I enjoy hating these things so I am not going to).

My boss at the time loved exactly those things and was desperately trying to motivate me into moving into the team by telling me what fun I would have making graphs out of all the numbers and finding all the little errors by sifting through mountains of data. I was close to death after every one of his motivation sessions.

All he had to do was understand where I was coming from rather than what he enjoys. Simply, at the time I had a vision of me being a great trainer. My identity was based on this and all of my career outcomes revolved round this vision. All my boss needed to say was all great trainers are good at training evaluation. If he had said that, nothing on earth would have kept me from moving in to the role. It was experience I didn't have and was important for my identity. AND I would have loved every minute of working in that department.

That's right. Despite saying I hate everything about that sort of work I would have loved working there. Because I would be learning and experiencing a whole new aspect of the training cycle that was making me a better trainer and therefore reinforcing the way I wanted to see myself.

Perceptual Positions & The Nature of Yet Another Reality

There were two separate and even conflicting realities and either could have been triggered by my manager. He chose one that made my life difficult only because he did not understand me enough to realise how he could have got me exceptionally motivated.

Jan is realising the same thing in her email. The organisational outcomes and personal outcomes from a situation do not need to be the same.

Your reality is only a matter of perspective and it can and does change. If my manager had been focused on my version of reality he might have seen the easy route to change it and create a new reality that gave the company what was needed and made me a happier man.

Objection Handling using Hypnotic Language Patterns

I have recently been sent an email from a guy I will refer to as Dr Tom. Dr Tom is a chiropractor and hypnotist and talks about certain types of resistance he gets from his clients. This gives me the opportunity to demonstrate some NLP language patterns that you can use to bypass resistance and refocus your client in the right direction. Here is the email in full:

Hi Rintu, I am very impressed with the first two lessons. I did notice in the first lesson you used the word "but" in a certain way, then in the second lesson you made specific instructions to use "and" instead of "but". I have not had a real good chance to study and contrast the reason and understand why this is so, but I will.

I am a chiropractor and certified hypnotist trying, after 10 years in business, to talk to people in a way that gets the importance of the adjustment across, and deliver a better understanding of what I do so that people will come in for healthcare instead of "bandaid" care, only when they are hurting. Unfortunately, that is what I instructed/taught people to do ever since I opened my office.

I am working out scripts based on lesson #2 to answer the question/comment I have gotten quite often in the past which is:

"Once you go to a chiropractor, you have to go forever; I just want the pain gone and to come back when it hurts."
Or
"Why should I bring my kids in, they're not old? They don't have back pain, why do you crack a kid's back?"

Most people don't have any idea of how important chiropractic care is, and I have not done a very good job of educating them. I have read dozens of books on hypnosis, NLP, Zig Zigler (way ahead of his time by the way, he talks about all of these principles before they called it NLP) and am reading blogs and talking to chiropractic coaches.

Your information is very much appreciated and I will let you know how it works. I want a win/win relationship with my patients. I know people will get more from what I do if I can explain it better and have sincere and convincing answers to questions like these.

Thank you, your information is better than most.
Dr. Tom

Below is an edited version of the email I sent back to Dr Tom with a few ideas for reframing the resistance.

NLP Objection Handling

Hi Tom,

Thanks for emailing. Your email sets up a lot of good questions and I would like to use it as the basis of an article for the techniques section of the website. In the meantime some short answers for you:

With relation to 'but' vs. 'and' the way you can start to latch on to what I do with them is to notice the phrase before the but/and. When I want people to forget the first bit and focus on the second I will tend to use 'but' and when I want them to connect the two phrases together I will use 'and'... for example:

"I have some bad news about your current health situation, but the good news is that it is all repairable."

"The good news is that you can have a great healthy spine and you will have to put some attention on maintaining that level once you have reached it."

If you go back to the agreement frame and redefine patterns you might find some answers such as this one below. And if you look through it you might find a whole lot of other patterns as well.

"I agree your kids are not old and the issue is not their age but their ongoing health and wellbeing as they grow up. Having good chiropractic care would mean they reduce the chances of ever having a bad back... I think most good parents have some worry about the health of their children, but the best are forward thinking enough to put preventative measures in place and that might give you more peace of mind. When would be a good time to book your son in for an initial examination?"

Tom, just remember this is for illustration only. I would not say this much out as a monologue and in such an adversarial way. My message would be the same patterns but delivered interactively as part of a conversation. Hopefully this will give you a couple of ideas of your own.

Cheers
Rintu

Covert Hypnosis in The Real World

The issue in these situations is not the resistance but the focus your client has on something that is not useful for them. In the case of Dr Tom's clients they are only focused on cure not prevention.

By widening the focus through such things as redefine patterns you are opening your client's mind to different opportunities. The issue is not their presenting problem but what would be the best solution.

The Key Secret To NLP Persuasion

Before I give you another example of reframing the issue here is the key to all persuasive language...

Rapport

Without rapport none of the ideas I am suggesting will work. My version of rapport is not the basic NLP 'matching and mirroring' thing; you need to pace your client's current experience and then lead them to a new way of thinking about the issue. We will discuss rapport in more depth later. Anyway, assuming you have a level of rapport, here is another example of the things I might say to Dr Tom's clients:

"The issue is not your bad back but are you prepared to allow your son to suffer the same problems as you in later life. Good preventative treatment now will mean his back, posture and general health will make him less likely to suffer the problem you are currently having."

And if I really wanted the parent nailed down about this issue before the statement above I might say something like:

"Are you already aware that children learn their adult behaviour by unconsciously modelling their parents? How much have you taught your son about how to have a bad back?"

Come back to this statement after a few more chapters to see the other patterns that are here.

Finally, another couple of quick examples that people have mailed in.

Not that I want to foment teenage rebellion but here is a great pattern from a guy to his parents, slightly edited from the original:

"I agree you want me home by ten o'clock and that is because you want to make sure I am home safe, what I would add is the issue is not whether I am home, but that I am safe… if I promise to text at ten then you know I am safe."

It didn't quite work, but top marks for effort. The real issue was about getting up the next morning ready for school, so unfortunately whilst the pattern was well formed it was operating on the wrong piece of leverage.

Here's one that *did* work.

> *"I agree it is work that needs to be done and that is why I suggest we leave it until we have enough time to do a quality job... The issue isn't just about getting it done, but getting it done well so that people will respond."*

A great job of getting out of being overloaded with extra work.

Let me know how else you are using these patterns. There is a whole world of people out there to play with, the issue isn't about learning patterns, it's about having fun with them, until they start really producing results.

Using Simple Words To Add & Delete Thoughts

Add, Delete and Qualify Different Statements That Don't Otherwise Have To Be Connected

This chapter is all about adding, deleting and joining thoughts. Why would you want to know how to do this? Perhaps you want to get a person to let go of their current thinking and move on to new ideas. The patterns you are using do this already, but what you are learning here is more flexibility... and what that means is you are creating more patterns of your own. This makes you more persuasive because you can start using your language instead of following my patterns blindly.

Using Simple Words To Increase Your Influence Over Others

We are going to look a little more at words like "and", "but" and "because." And as a special bonus we will also look at "yet." I love the first three words because they allow you to add, delete and qualify different statements that don't otherwise have to be connected, and "yet" gives motion to stuck states.

You might not see how this works just yet, but you will once we have discussed the basics and then you will be amazed at what you can do with a few words. I suspect you are getting a sense of how powerful these words are because you are noticing just how much movement I can create in this one paragraph alone. If you have not yet seen it re-read this paragraph and notice just how simply we can connect ideas. This works because of the powerful nature of the connecting words I am using. I know this is not very clear yet, but it will be once you have read through the rest of this chapter, and then you will be amazed at how simple it is.

There are lots of ways of using these words, but we are going to concentrate on giving people feedback or criticism because it is an application that is easy to see and, by looking at this area, you will easily be able to think of your own applications.

Let us start with the word "but". Have you ever been in a conversation that started something like, "I think you are a great guy, but..." Or perhaps, "You did a great piece of work, but...", and then the rest of the conversation is about how you can't do anything right or no one likes you?

The word "but" acts as a delete button to what came before and sets people up for the bad news that is supposed to follow. So an easy way of using these words is to put the bad news first and follow through with the good news.

Here's an example:

> *"That report had lots of mistakes, but the overall sense of it is great."*

Or

> *"No, you can't stay out past ten tonight, but the weekend is a different issue."*

That's straightforward enough so let's add "and" to the mix. The word "and" allows you to add a new thought and connect it to the first. So going back to those two examples we'll add a little more in...

> *"That report had a lot of mistakes, but the overall sense of it is great and how good are you going to feel when you have made all the corrections and everyone is telling you how good it is?"*

Or

> *"No, you can't stay out past ten tonight, but the weekend is a different issue and that is when you are going to have the most fun, isn't it?"*

Okay, so now you are getting the idea of how "but" and "and" work let us examine the word "yet". But before we do, did you notice how in the second example, by making it a question you are focusing the subject's mind in an entirely new direction?

"Yet" is a word that creates movement to stuck states. Just adding "yet" to the end of the phrase "I can't..." creates an opening for change. As a trainer and a coach I use this pattern a lot. Suppose a delegate on a course says something like "I can't understand this."

One of my stock replies starts with, *"That's right; you don't understand this yet..."* Remember the agreement frame we've looked at before and now I have added "yet" which creates movement.

The next part of my response involves the word "because." I love this word because it allows you to not only connect two ideas in a sentence but also say the first idea causes the second. The two ideas don't need to relate to each other although any plausible link obviously helps. I guess you might not understand this yet, that is because you might need to see an example for it to click into place. So let us go back to my response to the "I can't" statement:

> *"That's right, you can't understand this yet, that's because you have not yet thought about this in terms of your applications... and when you do that you will find it easy to understand."*

If you have not already done this yet, I suggest that you look through this lesson again just noticing the number of connections through "but", "and" and "because" that I have used. I think this is worth doing because as you notice them you will see just how easy it is to move ideas into and out of your subject's thoughts. Then all you need is a few simple thoughts on applications and you will be a master at this.

So here are a few examples:

> *"That report was really good because it is very readable and how much better are you going to feel about it when you have corrected all the spelling mistakes?"*

"I almost agree that you shouldn't have to go to bed yet and you could just get ready for bed now so you can go as soon as your TV programme has finished."

"You are right it is not easy to understand but how much better will you feel when you have studied it a little. I'm sure that you already see it will be easier and that is because you will understand it a little more."

"It does seem expensive but that is because we have not yet gone through the return on investment this product will give you and I am sure you will feel much better about it once we have. Shall we do that now, because I would want you to feel good about the product now?"

Finally a couple of examples that have been sent in...

"I knew it wasn't the greatest piece of work, but the issue was more about getting something done within the deadline, would you have preferred it to have been late?"

Good result for shifting the heavy amount of criticism that was just about to start flying her way.

"I agree it's scary, but think about how you will feel once it's done and out of the way. The issue is really about how brave you can be now."

Neuro Linguistic Parenting and talking your child into being brave at the dentist.

I invite you to notice how easy language patterns are becoming. It is because you are learning to construct a variety of patterns that are easy to use and formulate and within a few days you will be constructing great new patterns for yourself.

In the next chapter we will be looking at patterns of awareness and you will see some of the most powerful persuasion patterns ever. Suppose for a moment that there are two or three little words that you can use to make any statement true for the person listening. Do you already realise how much persuasive power you will have by learning to use these patterns?

Having The Confidence To Practice With Real People

What Do You Need To Say or Do To Be Really Comfortable Practicing With People?

Your next chapter is only a few pages away, so if you have not yet been throwing patterns out at random people then go and have some fun with the patterns you already have, because in the next chapter we will discuss an extremely powerful pattern that many NLPers gloss over.

Let Go of The Fear of Failure

For those of you that have not yet let go of the fear of failure and embraced the idea of learning through small steps and practice I have a couple of things for you.

Firstly, have you ever stumbled over your words, forgotten what to say or mumbled something incredibly dumb at anyone? Was anyone maimed, killed or injured as a result? Did anyone go to prison? I guess most of the time the biggest result was you getting embarrassed and repeating yourself with what you *wanted* to say. Just because you are practicing patterns doesn't mean that the world will come to an end because you stumble over your words.

Here is an exercise for you... Take a few patterns and just try them out... you get double points if you get them wrong, stumble over your words or do something incredibly stupid and embarrassing.

If anyone does get maimed, killed or goes to jail as a result of what you say then you are on your own... If you have that much power you don't need this book.

Usually at this point on a course someone starts talking about being caught out and I usually reply, "So what?" Unless you are trying to do something with bad intent does it really matter?

I tend to say something like:

> "That's right I am trying to bend you to my will, what do I need to say or do to enslave your mind and make you mindlessly do my bidding for the rest of your life?"

If you don't like that one here are a few more:

> "That's right I am practicing persuasive language patterns can I try a few more out on you?"

> "Yes, I am a Hypnotic Persuasion Skills Master, but if you find yourself with no trousers in the High Street squawking like a chicken it is because you have had too much to drink and nothing to do with me."

> "I thought it was you trying to persuade me? Where did you learn your patterns?"

> "That is quite a paranoid thought, but I have heard there are people out to get you."

> *"Yes, you caught me trying to get you to do what I think is best for you so kill me now for having your best interests at heart."*

I could go on, but the issue is not me coming up with more patter but you getting the idea that you can say anything and just move the conversation on.

The only time it gets to be an issue (outside of where you have some bad intent and in that case it is your own fault) is with controlling and manipulative people. Without fail they will start on you with their issues around control and manipulation. The standard one I get is, "NLP is very manipulative."

I have several responses but my usual is:

> *"And that is a very manipulative response, what are you trying to get me to say, do or think?"*

I then lead them through a redefine:

> *"The issue isn't manipulation but intent…"*

And then into a discussion about how all communications is manipulation and if they have an issue with *that* then they can put their own house in order by never speaking again. You might guess that I don't have much time for people that take this path.

Using Perceptual Positions To Create a More Persuasive Personality

Here is an exercise for you that will help you become more confident and persuasive. The exercise is a variant of perceptual positions and I mention it here only for those of you that like to know where this has come from.

I am not going to explain all the detail about perceptual positions itself as you can easily find this in almost every NLP book in existence and you only need to Google it to find out more. I am just going to give you the process.

The exercise is about building a representation of you as the ideal persuasion master and to be able to access the internal resources of this new hypothetical you. This works on the basis of learning from different perspectives as well as mental rehearsal and might even give you an action plan of how you want to develop. As an exercise this works with any sort of personality you wish to choose, for example being a good parent, inspiring leader or suave seducer... but for the purpose of the exercise I will talk about a persuasion master.

Firstly I would like you to remember a specific situation from the recent past where you did not perform as well as you would like. Remember there is a difference between doing and practicing, so for the moment, while you are learning this exercise pick something small and relatively insignificant. As you get better at this pick situations that have more impact.

Notice the way you behaved, your body language, what you said, how you said it and how all that contributed to the result you got. Now I want you to think about what values, beliefs and thought processes you must have gone through to create this behaviour.

Now imagine a new you acting the way that you would have liked in that situation. Again notice everything, the body language, what you said and how you said it. Step over to this new version of you and step into the body. From the inside, notice what it is like to be this person, understand what kind of beliefs and values they hold to be this way. Notice what it feels like to act in this way and do the things they are doing.

Once you have spent a few minutes enjoying this step out of that body and back to yourself. Ask yourself what you have learnt from this part of the exercise.

Next I want you to take an observer position where you can visualise both the old and the new you. In essence you are watching the current version of you watching the new version of you. From this perspective, notice the differences between the two and start coaching the old you into becoming the new you... yes you will be talking to yourself and feel free to do this aloud on the train going home... it ensures you get a seat for all three versions of you.

It is important that from the observer position you are emotion free, non-judgemental and just encouraging the old you into changing. You might even be able to work out an action or practice plan to develop into the new version of you... or ideally you might even notice that you have always been the new version of you and it is just a change of perspective that allows you to suddenly find yourself being like this. Do this however it works best for you.

Finally you want the old and new versions of you to merge together doing what you would like to do in that given situation.

This will work well for a general concept of the new version of you but works even better if you can localise it to specific situations where you want to act differently.

It sounds like a long-winded exercise but it takes more to explain than to do. Also the more you do it the more you will find yourself just doing it instinctively without much conscious thought. Remember we are dealing with persuasion skills but you can use this general exercise for any behaviour you want to change.

Learn to Talk to Yourself to Develop Self-Esteem

Many people talk to themselves... and if you don't then I suggest you start practicing having a little voice in your head. There is a great benefit here. Imagine having someone that is always thinking the best for you whispering good things in your ear 24/7. Having that voice is really useful. The issue for some is that the voice they have doesn't say good things and criticises when things don't work and it calls them bad names using language you don't use in front of your mother.

The thing is now you are learning about language patterns you can start creating patterns and deal with this voice as an objection. Alternatively you can make patterns from the things you would like to say to yourself in your head and start practicing persuading yourself that you are the person you want to be. Either way you are developing your confidence, self-esteem and practicing your language patterns all at the same time.

Awareness Patterns

Reading This You Will Quickly Notice How Powerful These Patterns Are

Y ou are just about to find one of the most powerful NLP language patterns in existence. And hardly any NLP Practitioners really know how to use awareness patterns...

Even better than that, you will get to see pacing and leading language that will show you how to 'future pace' these patterns so they spread out through time... could you imagine what it would be like if every time you flicked a light switch or settled down to watch TV you suddenly found yourself thinking about the thoughts I have put in your head.

Thoughts about becoming an even more skilful persuader, through understanding, practice and imagination.

Okay that was a blatant demo of the patterns from the next few chapters but I invite you to notice how strong this hypnotic pattern can be... and they are all here for you in this book. The key is practice... so read, understand and then do.

I invite you to notice the power of awareness patterns. These are little known and incredibly powerful covert NLP patterns you can learn.

These patterns are some of the simplest and easiest to use, but once you understand how to use them you will suddenly realise how easy and powerful they are. Unless I am completely wrong and you obviously don't realise how easy they are. But in either case you will find them very powerful.

Have you noticed how some things are just taken for granted? What I mean is that sometimes a person can say things and what they say is never questioned. If there are patterns that allow you to do this, are you aware of how powerful they would be? We are talking about awareness patterns and you might already be noticing that they really can be that powerful.

NLP Awareness Patterns

Awareness patterns in language are words like; "notice", "realise", "experience", "see" and "aware". They are really powerful because everything after the word is presupposed as true. Let's just deconstruct what makes the pattern so powerful.

I could just make a statement and tell you that awareness patterns are powerful. But this is very obvious and subject to challenge. I could ask you if you think awareness patterns are powerful. But this gives you the option to agree or disagree. But if I were to say something like, *"By reading this sentence you will start to notice how powerful awareness patterns are."* The second half of the sentence is presupposed to be true. If anyone were to challenge the sentence they will usually challenge the first half i.e. "How does reading that sentence make me more aware of the power?" There is still a presupposition of the power in the challenge.

Just notice how you can ramp this up by changing the statement into a question. For example, *"Do you realise how powerful awareness patterns are?"* This is a closed question and whether you answer yes or no the issue is that you are reflecting on your *realisation* not on how powerful the pattern is. Is this really sneaky stuff or what?

Having read the previous paragraph I invite you to notice how flexible and easy this is to use... and are you starting to experience the power of these patterns? Holding this book, reading through this chapter means you are already seeing dozens of applications. If you haven't already noticed several ways of using this yet, it is because you need a couple of examples to get you going. So here are a few more rather clever awareness patterns.

'Awareness Patterns' Examples

A fairly typical sales conversation that I have had in the past might go:

> *"Are you already aware of the power an NLP Practitioner course will give you?"*

A "yes" answer would be perfect, but let us say the prospect says "No."

I would just respond with:

"I agree you are not yet aware and that's because we haven't yet been through the course content as it would apply directly to you. Shall we do that now?"

Firstly, just check how many of the patterns we have already discussed are embedded in to these two sentences. As you read through them just notice how simple it is to integrate this sort of persuasive language into your everyday life.

Secondly, are you also aware of the fact that the power of a NLP Practitioner course is completely presupposed in all of this, i.e. the question of this being useful for the prospect is never challenged, just whether they have realised it or not.

Here is something I might use in a training room. "It may seem like a complex subject, but as we start to go through the material and you learn some of the techniques you might already start to become aware of how easy this is to put into practice."

Having just read this paragraph and looked through some of the previous material you could have noticed already another pattern I use a lot in training called pacing and leading. This is a subject we will come back to later as a way of getting agreement and buy in from an unconscious perspective. But for the moment just notice how easy it is to bring awareness patterns into your normal conversation.

Are you seeing how easy it is to start to think of examples for yourself? Here is a rapport building pattern for flirting, networking or anywhere you want to build more rapport.

Once you have a level of rapport and connection with someone you might say something like, *"It's been good to meet you and I don't know if you have noticed how much rapport we have got. It just means we will get on even better when we... (meet again/start working together/wake up next to each other etc. etc.)"* This example contains a future pace statement which is something we will come back to in another lesson along with anticipation loops.

How would this be for setting up a paranoia programme? *"Have you noticed how much people are talking about you behind your back? ... Oh, you haven't noticed yet. Sorry, I've said too much. Just forget I mentioned it."* And then walk away. I'm not serious about developing nasty patterns but I just wanted to share this with you to demonstrate how simple, quick and powerful this pattern can be.

Anyway have a look through this lesson again just to notice how much I have used this pattern. As you read through it and notice the patterns you will become more amazed at how simple it is to use and in the next chapter you will laugh at how much more power you can add when we discuss pacing and leading patterns.

Your homework, as usual, is to write out a half dozen patterns and say them to someone. Let go of any outcomes, just flap your gums at people with these new patterns. Remember build some rapport; speak a little slower and a little lower. As you get more used to talking and thinking in this way you will be amazed at how much more influence you have with people.

Rapport ... More Than Mimicry?

What the NLPers Don't Tell You About Rapport

This book is about persuasive language, but no persuasion topic is complete without some mention and discussion of rapport. Getting into the heads of your subjects and really understanding how they are thinking is vital.

Remember the key to influencing skills is to understand the benefit to the subject for doing what you want them to do and then being able to present that to them in a way that they can understand. With this in mind here is a short and incomplete discussion on rapport with a few ideas you can use straight away.

You will find lots written about rapport. As such the main body of this interlude is all about how to really create great rapport quickly and easily. We will talk about how many NLP Practitioners get it wrong, the key ingredients to get it right and a specific process to take charge of a conversation. I will show you one specific technique that many of my graduates have used to get better jobs, relationships and sales.

What is Rapport? A Basic Explanation

First, let us define rapport and discuss how so many NLPers get it so wrong. For a more full discussion on the standard view of rapport and all the misconceptions out there just type the word into a search engine. You will find a lot written and I would rather cover different ground. For our purpose it is just a method for increasing the responsiveness of your subject. This often involves some sort of liking or mutual respect but doesn't have to.

As this is about influence and persuasion we don't just want to build rapport but also to take control and lead the conversation to where you want it to go.

Standard NLP Rapport Process

The standard NLP approach is all about matching and mirroring body language, breathing, words and anything else your subject lets you do. The basic idea being that people like people that are like themselves. This happens on an unconscious level and by matching or mirroring a subject you gain this rapport. At a foundation level this works, but there are several issues with it.

- Matching and mirroring is more a rapport *indicator* than a rapport *maker*.
- This is supposed to happen on an unconscious level.
- You are not leading your subject; in fact you are spending all your attention just pacing them.
- Whilst you are doing all of this aren't you supposed to be in a conversation as well?

I love meeting new NLP Practitioners because I tilt my head at odd angles, scratch myself in private and delicate areas and develop strange facial twitches whilst watching them desperately trying to mechanically match and mirror my body language. As you get more practised you can get them to fall off chairs by leaning and hyperventilate through constantly changing your breathing patterns.

Whilst we are talking about NLP Practitioners can I recommend using this phrase when you meet them and they tell you proudly that they are certified Practitioners of NLP and who they trained with:

> *"The issue is not the certificate but how well you can use the skills, how specifically do you use covert hypnotic persuasion techniques to get results?"*

Then just sit back and watch them squirm. Often they will make the excuse of taking just what they need and they didn't need the language, or my personal favourite, "I use it all the time unconsciously."

At this point you know you could have tremendous fun messing with their minds, but to be nice gently point out that the subject is called Neuro-Linguistic Programming. They have been on a course where they can't properly say they use one third of the material based on the title. Then point them at this book and let them know that for a modest investment of time and energy they can get a proper understanding of some powerful patterns.

A good NLP Practitioner training course will show you a number of great rapport techniques that really work and you can use in any situation. Because this is a little outside the scope of this book we will focus on easy foundation concepts that will work anywhere and with any situation, as well as a specific process that lets you covertly take charge in one to one circumstances. But this is a simplistic view and you can get some ideas of where you can find out more in the resources section.

Rapport in One Easy Step

The quickest, easiest and simplest way to gain rapport is to assume you have it already. In most situations this works perfectly. If you imagine the person you are talking to is a very dear and close friend, then the way you speak, your body language and your attitude towards them is very subtly different from normal. On an unconscious level you will be sending signals that the subject will respond to and you will be leading them into feelings of familiarity and responsiveness.

Also if you get outside your head and in to the head of the person you are speaking to. What I mean is start to imagine what they are seeing, hearing and feeling. Think about how they are representing the world to themselves and what values and beliefs they have to have to behave the way they do. All of this is building empathy.

Obviously on your Practitioner course we will build rapport techniques that have a lot more sophistication and allow you to, for example:

- Covertly change your subject's emotions
- Build rapport with groups
- Implant suggestions

And a huge range of other things but they all start with the same basic premise of assuming you already have rapport.

Next let's talk about a specific process that covertly lets you take complete control of a conversation and is ideal for situations such as job interviews, sales or networking.

Covert Conversation Control

Here is a specific technique that allows you to take control of a conversation whilst increasing the subject's responsiveness and creating feelings of warmth, familiarity and friendliness. It works well in most situations but has a special effect with people you are meeting for the first time. I will explain it in the context of a job interview because it is the perfect situation for this technique. You can then adapt the process for any situation you care to choose.

Before I get into the guts of the process I would like you to follow a little thought experiment with me. Imagine you are walking down the street when you see an old and dear friend that you have not seen for years. Let me take you through a typical process that you might go through:

1. You look at them hesitantly not sure it is really them.

2. You make eye contact as you realise it is them.

3. You slowly grow a smile across your face as you start thinking about good memories you have shared and how great it is to see them.

4. At the same time you will start feeling good inside, just notice that the feeling starts small and takes time to grow in intensity.

5. You will then step forward confidently, with your hand out to shake hands warmly.

This might not be exactly what you would do, but it should have similarities and this is what I would like you to do when meeting someone for the first time.

Here is what is happening and why this is a good way of meeting people. By reacting to people as if they are a close friend you set up your unconscious signals in a way that radiates warmth, confidence (you are confident when you are with your friends) and familiarity. Outside of their conscious awareness, this is what the other person will pick up on and react to.

I pointed out being hesitant at the beginning, slowly smiling and the feeling starting and growing. This is because people notice things changing much more than a static device. Simply, you would notice someone much more if they started from a neutral expression to smiling than if they were just smiling or just neutral. Also this sequence of events is taking you, and them, from neutral to liking. In NLP jargon it is pacing and leading them.

The smile and putting your hand out to shake has other benefits as well. We are socialised to smile at each other and to shake hands when one is offered. What has happened here is you have made a gesture and they have responded by smiling and shaking your hand. In simple terms you have asked them to do something and they have done it. You have covertly taken control of the situation and the conversation and have built rapport on a deep level. From here you can use your hypnotic language, influencing processes and all the good stuff you are learning to great effect.

Obviously there are stronger, more powerful and sophisticated techniques for building rapport and gaining unconscious control of a conversation. But I have taught this process to many job candidates and whilst it doesn't always guarantee a good interview I have yet to find anyone saying it did not make a significant difference.

Now for those of you that are not in the job hunting market, let me know how many different environments and situations you have already found to use this process with.

Pacing & Leading

**A Doorway To Unconscious Persuasion...
Implanting Assumptions Into The Heads of
Others Through Pace & Lead Statements**

I know if you are sitting comfortably, reading this line you will find this lesson of great use because you will be able to simply move people in a direction. As you think about that and consider the contexts where you could use this knowledge can you think about feeling excited about the results you will get?

Particularly when you start combining various patterns...

Anyway, without further ado, here is the lesson.

We are half way through the book and that means you are aware of how much has changed with the way that you think about language. Having looked through some of these lessons and thought about how you would use the information you will have noticed how easy it is to become more persuasive.

Sitting comfortably, reading these word means you are ready for this lesson that is all about pacing and leading. We briefly mentioned pacing and leading earlier, you will have noticed I have connected them to awareness patterns and you might already be seeing how easy they are to integrate together to make your patterns even more explosively powerful.

Pace & Lead

So let's get on to what pacing and leading patterns are, what makes them useful and how we use them. I assume you are curious about these patterns and I am excited about how useful you will find them so let us start learning about these patterns.

When you make statements that are absolutely true for the listener they will unconsciously build agreement with you. This is a little bit like the flip side of the agreement frame that we discussed in an earlier lesson. So if you do this enough your subject is happily sitting there agreeing with your comments and then you add in something that you want them to believe to be true that moves them in the direction you want them to move in. In old style sales techniques this used to be called building yes sets, but we are going to use this in a much more subtle and powerful way.

Old Style Hypnotic Sale Technique

Sales people used to phrase their questions to always get a yes answer from the prospect so that when they came to asking for the sale the prospect had already got used to saying yes and would find it much easier. An over exaggerated version might look like this:

"We have spent some time discussing the product? You have seen how you benefit from it? We have gone through your requirements and discussed how well the product meets your needs? Are you ready to buy now?"

If the first three questions are answered with a "yes" then you have started to build a pattern and it is easier for the prospect to say "yes" to the fourth question.

Hypnotists and hypnotherapists use the same concept to send people in to trance. Here is a typical hypnosis trance script:

> *"You are sat feeling the weight of your body sinking into the chair, listening to my voice talking to you as you start to slip further into trance."*

Notice that the first two are verifiable sensory experiences that would be going on for the subject right then and there, whilst the third part of the statement is phrased the same way it is actually a command to go further in to trance.

Pacing and leading statements work exactly in the same way. We generally use three statements because it is an easy number to keep track of and the most common convincer strategy is three. That is to say the majority of people prefer to get things three times before being convinced, taking action etc. This is not true of everyone just that most people respond to cycles of three.

The structure of a good pace and lead statement then is two statements that are completely and verifiably true followed by a statement that is plausible and leading to where you want your client to go. For example, sitting comfortably, reading these words means that you are already having ideas about how you can use this pattern. The first two statements are true and the third moves you to where I want you to go.

Before we get in to a few applications and examples I would like to pause for a moment and talk about the phrase "and that means." This is another linking phrase that connects two statements that are not necessarily connected but you would like them to be. I like "and that means" statements because I can use them to connect anything to anything else. For example, since you are reading this statement it means that you are clever, intelligent and witty enough to understand how to use these phrases and that means you see the value of them and obviously this means that you want to take out your wallet and hand my large sums of money for my insight… and so on.

So, having read up to this point and realising the power of pacing and leading statements you are keen to see a few examples and that means you are ready to use them in your daily life.

Pace & Lead Examples

MANAGEMENT

"You have worked in this department for six months; produced some great work and that means you are ready to take on this very important project."

TRAINING

"Having booked on this course and turned up at this venue means that you are really keen to learn."

DATING

"Sat here, having dinner with you and building a great relationship makes us feel really good."

The last example is also using, in NLP jargon terms 'process based language' and a switch in 'referential index'. These are a couple of things that we will come back to later, along with building anticipation loops.

RECRUITMENT

"You have seen the job specification, replied with a great CV and so must be relaxed enough to give me an informative interview."

SQUARING UP FOR A RAISE

"I've worked for you now for four months and in that time I have increased the sales in the company by 50%, so you know that it is important for me to be recognised for my achievements."

BEING INTERVIEWED

A very strong approach that would need good rapport...

"Having read my CV and listened to me in this interview when will you be deciding that I am the ideal candidate for the role?"

NLP Hypnotic Language: 'Future Pace'

This last example uses a pattern that I call a 'future pace'. You will be using future pace statements to increase anticipation, focus people on results and change their thoughts and behaviour, on both a conscious and unconscious level. But that is something we can come back to later.

Now that you have read through this lesson and seen a few examples you are ready to write out a few patterns of your own. If you were to think about a few contexts where you can use this and practice saying out loud a few patterns you will, within a day or so, be using pacing and leading statements to move people to where you want them to go. Have you already realised how much more influencing power you have once you start combining all these patterns? This issue isn't about learning these patterns but looking back from the future where you are already using them fluently and noticing how you are doing that.

Anyway, find a few pacing and leading patterns, some unsuspecting innocents and language pattern them through the floor. Let me know the results.

Results of Pacing & Leading

Imagine the results you are going to get as you are assimilating all these new ideas... Here are some examples from my students:

TEACHER TO PUPIL

"Misbehaving and not doing your homework just means you will fail, but the real issue is how you can get a good school report. Imagine how your parents will react when I give them a glowing report next week when we meet. All you need to do is..."

MANAGER TO EMPLOYEE

After being knocked back for promotion:

"I agree you should have got the job and would add the real issue is how we can turn this around in your favour. Right now I understand you are upset and a little angry and that means you care a lot about this company and your role in it. Why don't we book some time next week to talk about how we are going to help you move forward in to the role that you want."

DRIVER TO POLICE OFFICER

"I agree officer, I was going a little faster than the speed limit and would add that I am so keen to get home that I didn't see the speed limit. You standing here, talking to me is a great reminder of public safety. What do I need to say or do to convince you that I am normally very conscious of speed limits and this is the only reminder that you need to give me?"

This last example is great for two reasons. Firstly thinking of it on the spot and also because of the terrific conditional close at the end, so well done... and for the rest of you he got away without a ticket.

Hypnotic Language: Conditional Close

Before we start on the next section let's spend a couple of minutes on conditional closes. Please note that for the sales people I have a slightly different meaning for 'conditional closes' than is usually meant in sales training. But a question like, *"What do I need to say or do for you to do (x)?"* is great because the *answer* is the information you need to get the result you are asking for. I think the pattern is straight forward and doesn't need any more explaining except to ask you the question:

"What do you need to do for you to apply this pattern straight away?"

The issue is not the answer to that question but the fact that you are thinking about all the different situations where this would be a good pattern to use. I hope you have realised that because you are thinking through the question and reading the rest of this paragraph that it is becoming very easy to integrate new patterns. Can you imagine the results you are going to get as you are assimilating all these new ideas? Think about where you will be in six months or a year when you are looking back towards now as the start of becoming a really magnificent persuader.

Another Approach to Pacing and Leading

Now you have learned about pacing and leading, looked at some examples and have been thinking about and trying some of it out for a few days, let me tell about other approaches to pacing and leading.

On my NLP Persuasion Skills for CV Writing and Job Interviews we look at this pacing and leading thing as the introduction to the interview. Whereas in most interview situations the interviewer leads the conversation my approach is to create a situation where the interviewee has complete covert control of the whole process whilst still maintaining rapport.

This is done through attitude, body language and artful answers to questions. Within the first two minutes an interviewee should have rapport and covert control if they are using my system. Even if you are not specifically looking for a new role, in how many situations would you find this skill useful?

Over the next two chapters we will look at some techniques where you can, by asking the right question take your subject on any journey you want them to go on. Now, is that a powerful skill to have?

Since we were talking about job interviews consider the implications of asking an interviewer a question like, *"If I were doing a great job, what results would you be seeing me achieve?"* If you don't "get it" that's okay, read through the next two chapters and then come back to this page.

Using Internal Representations To Create an Unconscious Direction of Thought

Say What You Want Them To Think

I hope you are ready for this influence and persuasion lesson. We are looking at internal representations and how you can force a direction of thought on anyone by what you say... this happens normally all the time. But by knowing what is happening when we speak to each other you will never have a normal conversation again. So welcome to my world.

The real power comes when you combine this idea with presuppositional questions. Can you imagine what it will be like when, just by asking a question, you set a direction and flow to a person's thoughts? Don't get too excited about it because that is the next chapter and we need to focus on this one first. So if you really want to get to grips with this lesson and put down the fundamentals the section on questioning becomes even more powerful.

The Key to Unconscious Persuasion Techniques...
Say What You Want Them to Think

In this chapter we are going to be talking more about leading. Specifically, how to lead the imagination. So first let us look at some ideas on what happens inside someone's head when you speak to them.

Your unconscious mind has to make an internal representation of anything we say for us to make sense of the sentence. For example, if I were to say, "John saw the mountain behind the house," you have to make an internal representation of John, a mountain and a house. If I were to say to you, "John didn't see the mountain behind the house because John, the mountain and the house don't exist," you still have to make the same internal representations. What you can take from this is that to make sense of what is said you have to make an internal representation of it.

Here is a slightly more complex situation. Notice the difference between these two statements:

1. *"Understanding this concept is hard."*

2. *"Understanding this concept is not easy."*

They both carry the same logical meaning but the second has a different set of representations. This is the idea that has been through a lot of the patterns we have discussed so far. I just haven't talked about this idea with you until now.

Now we can take this concept and develop it into leading the imagination. When I use words like "imagine", "consider" and "suppose"; or phrases like "What if…", "How about…" or "Think about…", I am giving you a direct command to use your imagination in the direction I want you to be thinking about. For a moment consider the benefits of getting your subject to think about the things you want them to think about. How useful would it be if you could do this?

Did you notice how sneaky this way of thinking really is? Just by saying the right things I can force the internal representation on you without you having any choice except… by refusing to listen.

Whist this is only a short couple of paragraphs there is something really fundamental in this so please allow me to summarise. Just by speaking, YOU force internal representations on to the listeners and by using particular words you can get them to imagine particular situations. The fact that you are doing this allows you to send the listener's mind in a particular direction.

Now that you know this, how many different ways can you think of using it?

Consider the value you could get from learning how to think differently about language. Perhaps you might be thinking about all the influence you can have over people and how you can get them to do more for you. Or you might be thinking of how to attract new clients, partners or prospects. Where would you get the most benefit from influencing and persuading people? I wouldn't want you to get too excited about it because there is some great material coming in the next chapter that will make this concept work even more powerfully.

In the next chapter we will be talking about using questions to lead the imagination and how we can use questions to create a strong emotional response. How would it be if you could do this already? What I mean by that is how excited can you get about learning questioning techniques that will get your prospect to shift their thinking towards where you want them to go? Would this be a useful skill to have?

Anyway, that is for the next chapter, for the moment let's think about how you are practicing patterns and routines. Imagine that you spent ten minutes a day for the next thirty days thinking up situations and how you can use your language differently to have more effect. Remember this is not actually doing anything differently, just thinking about how you would do it differently. If you did this, would it make a difference to the way that you act? I suspect it might, but I would like you to be sure of this by doing it.

Before reading on find a few people to flap your gums at. Shift their thoughts in different directions and leave them in a better place than you found them. If you can imagine doing this, how much better will you feel when you are looking back from having already done it?

Covert Hypnosis Example

It doesn't get any better than this...

Some people have baggage about NLP and conversational hypnosis thinking that it is manipulative and being used for bad purposes. The truth is, people with this sort of baggage are really telling you something about themselves, about their fears and even more about the direction their minds think in. As such I think there is value pausing for a few moments to think through some of the issues.

Are Hypnotic Language Patterns Manipulative?

Of course they are... all communications is manipulative. And people asking this question are usually trying to manipulate you into thinking that it's a bad thing and that we should all be like them.

I am only talking to you to be heard, amongst my many other agendas, such as seeking approval, selling courses and wanting to be understood. The issue is not manipulation but intent. In the same way as with any tools, you can use them with good intent helping yourself and others or by mistake, negligence or intent use them to harm. The tool is not the issue, just your intent when using it.

A little while ago I was sent a perfect example of a set of language patterns from Dr Tom. I am not going to explain the patterns because you will find them out for yourself from the material you have read through so far.

There are several sets of patterns going through this that I don't think Dr Tom is even aware of, but anyone who mails me with a good analysis of all the things going on in this example will get published on my website and possibly win some sort of a prize. Anyway here is Dr Tom's email in full as a perfect example of when to use a set of patterns, perfect delivery of those patterns and a perfect result. It really doesn't get better than this. Here is his email in full...

Hi Rintu,

Thank you again for providing such great and useful information.

My daughter came home from school with a low test grade (a 73). We have to sign off on all of her tests, (she is an excellent student) and I could tell she was a little nervous and uncomfortable/upset about showing me this one. I said to her:

"Sweetheart (she is 12 years old), I agree that this is not a very good grade, but you have made the Honor Roll for the past three semesters, you are a very smart girl, and I am very proud of you.

"The issue isn't how you did on this one test, but how excellent you have done in all of your other classes, you have a perfect attendance record and you have excelled in band (she plays the saxophone), chorus, softball, and basketball. And after we go over this test together, you will know the material as well as anyone who scored an A on the test, and that's what's really important, isn't it?

"I love you and know you will do better the next time."

Well, she went from being nervous and worrying that I would be disappointed in her, to beaming with confidence and being proud of herself. She gave me a big hug and a kiss and said, "Thanks dad, I love you."

It doesn't get any better than that.

Thanks Rintu.

Sincerely,
Dr. Tom

Questions Are The Answer

How Excited Would You Get If You Learned How To Use Questions To Lead People The Way You Want Them To Go?

Are you ready for the most powerful chapter yet? How would it be if you could set a direction of thought for anyone simply by asking a question?

How excited would you get at the prospect of creating an emotional state in your subject through simple questions?

Would you like to find out how?

When I was writing this section I got more and more excited about the whole prospect of sharing this with you… the sort of excitement that is a slow burn, you start with a little itch of curiosity, wondering where this is leading and as you get further into it you start to feel the rise of excitement when you start thinking of some basic language patterns and then you suddenly see all the applications and how it is changing your life. Like me, reading this through, wondering what the lesson contains you might already be feeling excited about the lesson… so without any more preamble here it is.

The Key to Hypnotic Persuasion… ask people to think the way you want them to think…

We have a lot to cover so let's just leap boldly straight into the idea. We are going to cover one of the most powerful trance techniques you will ever discover. You will find that the material we cover here will allow you to dramatically change people's states easily.

Why Would You Want To Change a Person's Trance State?

I am sure you can think of some obvious times where you might want to change the emotions in another person so let me give you the less obvious. All beliefs, decisions and thoughts have an emotional content to them... sometimes large, often so small we don't necessarily know they are there. But if you follow the idea then the next step that follows is that, if you can change the emotion then you can change the belief, thought or idea.

Reading this and thinking it through will bring you examples where you have done things based on the emotions of the moment. Ever made decisions when you were happy, sad, angry (insert favourite emotion here) and known it would have been different if you were in a different mood? How about your beliefs about yourself and the world about you, do they change dependant on the mood you are in?

Having thought about it you now know the truth of the matter. And you are already realising how powerful it is to be able to change the mood of the person you are talking to. Is it worth finding out how to do this?

Sensory Based NLP Language: Developing Process Based Hypnotic Language Patterns

A quick recap of the last chapter before we move into patterns, scripts and questions. The last golden nugget was that when you speak to someone they form an internal representation of what it is that you are speaking about. They have to do this to make sense of the sentence.

If I were to say to you, *"Don't get excited about the idea,"* you have to form an internal representation of getting excited about the idea to make sense of the sentence. So now all I have to do is get you to experience this a little more.

I might make a statement like:

> *"When I get a really good idea I start feeling a little fluttery feeling in my stomach that starts to move up towards my chest as I start to think of all the things that I can do with the new concept... and that is how you know you have got a good idea..."*

You might notice in this statement I have given you instructions on how to feel when you have a good idea. And guess what you have to try it on and see if it works, just to understand what I am saying. So now I can start to layer the process into your mind.

Did you also notice that I shifted from "I" statements to a "you" statement. In NLP jargon terms this is called a 'shift of referential index'. People rarely notice it and you will find a lot of people use it in natural speech... and it is a brilliant way of starting a conversation talking about yourself and ending talking about them without anyone noticing. Consider the following:

> *"When I first started thinking about language this way I had that fluttering feeling in my stomach, the type you get when you know that there is a brilliant idea just tickling at the back of your mind. And as I thought about it some more, thinking of all those places you can use the idea and how it will make a difference, you can start to feel it moving up through your chest, getting more intense with all the opportunities it opens up for you. Now, I wouldn't expect you to get this excited about it until you realise how powerful this concept is."*

Let me ask you, are you getting to realise how powerful this concept is yet? Do we need to go through a few examples and scripts to fully realise the power, beauty and elegance of you doing this? But let me not give you that until the end, because there is something else that I want to share that makes this even more powerful, adaptable and fun to use.

NLP Questions Are The Answer

If I say to you, *"Feel curious now,"* you have to form the internal representations, but you don't have to connect with them in any way.

If I say to you, *"When I feel curious I have a buzzing in my head and I feel drawn into the subject with a sort of itch that you just can't scratch, having to find out more."* I am giving you instructions on *how* to feel curious and you have to try on the internal representations, you might be closer than the first example, but you still do not need to connect.

If I were to ask you, *"How do you know when you are feeling immensely curious?"* you have to go inside to find the answers and do the process.

If I were to say to you, *"When I feel curious I have a buzzing in my head and I feel drawn into the subject with a sort of itch that you just can't scratch, having to find out more. How close is that to the way you feel when you are immensely curious?"* to answer the question you have to try on both and compare the results. Now I am getting you to access your feelings.

Now you have four ways of accessing a person's feelings from least to strongest:

1. Give them the internal representations, "You might find this interesting".

2. Give them a process for the feelings, "When I get interested it is because you suddenly see all the exciting possibilities and you can imagine all the new ways of thinking and the feeling starts to rise and become more intense."

3. Ask them questions, "How do you know when you are getting interested in a subject?"

   OR

4. A combination of all three:

   "I don't know if you will find this subject interesting. Certainly when I first came upon the concept I suddenly found myself thinking of loads of applications and my interest turned to major excitement as you thought through all the applications, it was like a heat rising up through my chest as I came up with more and more ideas. How do you know when your interest changes to pure excitement?"

The hardest thing about hypnotic and NLP language patterns is not to laugh as you are going through them with people. You will notice the state changes they go through, you will feel strange as you hear them agree with you and see them doing what you want. And you would expect that they would notice... Truth is, sometimes they do and they do it anyway because if you get this right they will feel good about it.

Now are you ready for some examples?

The examples that follow use a lot of the ideas that we have talked about in previous lessons as well as the concepts above. You might want to spend some time reading through these and doing a little bit of analysis. If this is the case, spend a few moments running through the internal representations the subject or audience would have to go through based on this script.

But remember that to really do this any justice you have to also focus on nonverbal communication – so there are some cues for that as well [in square brackets].

TRAINER WITH THE OPENING OF A DULL SUBJECT

[Starting real slow and picking up pace to real fast over the first two paragraphs… start sitting down and get up part the way through the first two paragraphs – all of this gives the impression of more energy and excitement.]

I don't expect you to get really excited about (x). It's not a particularly engaging subject, but when I was doing the research for this course I came across a couple of ideas that could revolutionise the way we work. Now that was something I could get excited about, do you have that fluttery feeling inside when you know there is something exciting just about to happen? That was how I felt when I started to think through some of the implications. You suddenly start to think of ideas, possibilities and how much better we can do things and you can get all that from a couple of the ideas we are going to cover this morning.

[Very suddenly back to slow again] *But that's to come a little later, first let me start with an overview of the day...*

[This is also an anticipation loop because the trainer does not let them know what, where or when in the morning these bits are coming. We will cover anticipation loops in a future chapter and you will be amazed at how powerfully they can work. Look out for it.]

MEETING SOMEONE FOR THE FIRST TIME - DATING

We could ask simple questions to find out about each other, but I am more interested in the passion in people's lives. You know the sort of thing when you feel the excitement rise and you just have to act on impulse... what things are you really [stress and draw this word out... reeaallly] *passionate about?*

NETWORKING

Same as flirting only more work relevant...

We could ask simple questions to find out about our roles and companies, but I am more interested in the passion in people's lives. You know the sort of thing when you rush in to the office feeling the excitement rise because you are going to do something great. What things really [stress and draw this word out... reeaallly] *excite you about your job?*

JOB INTERVIEW

When asked if you have any questions at the end of the interview…

I love working for companies where you can get excited about new developments. They don't have to be part of my role, just knowing the company is growing in new directions is an excitement you can feel getting more intense as I come into work each day. What developments in the company get you really excited? [Notice the sequence of internal representations here YOU can get excited as I come into work… this is real sneaky or what?]

SALES

I suspect that you sometimes get a feeling when you know you are buying the right thing. I know when I am doing it because I get a good feeling about the person I am talking to, I listen to all the benefits of the product and then I can see myself having fun using it… It's then you can start to feel very excited about buying the right thing for you. How do you know this is the right product for you? [Big assumptive close here… you could soften the last line by replacing the "do" with "would". Also a great question because they will either give you the feelings or their convincer strategy that you will need to fill for them to buy.]

Are you starting to get the idea? Read through some of the previous chapters looking for the places where I have used this process, have a look through the techniques section of the website and then have a look through this lesson again as well. You will find the whole thing littered with examples.

One final, but exceptionally important point. If you are installing a state in someone else you have to have rapport with them and you have to start to go in to the state yourself. Think about someone not getting excited when they are talking about something that is exciting and you will notice that it doesn't fit and couldn't work. Conversely have you ever noticed that you can get carried away with another's excitement when they are in full flow?

Hypnotic NLP Exercise

The issue is not about knowing about ideas, but is really about how you are going to use them. So, right now, think on the difference between knowing how to use the idea and going out to practice with it. What do you have to say or do so you just run into a couple of situations and practice on those mere mortals out in the world that don't know the implications of language the way you do?

As you are thinking about that questions and searching for some answers you might suddenly find yourself just writing out a few patterns and checking the internal representations the subject might have to go through.

You might then think of a few questions that accelerated the process and then imagine using those patterns. The issue is not using them but thinking through, in detail, where, when and how. Even in retrospect, reliving situations where you didn't use the patterns but could have and imagining how you could have had a huge benefit.

I would invite you to notice that the more you become familiar with these patterns the more they just seem to become a natural part of your life and you just naturally speak differently because of it.

Next we will talk about conversation management, the strategic approach to persuasion and how to accelerate your results.

Now, none of these things may seem very exciting, but what if I were to suggest that you can be exceptionally fast at developing your persuasive skills? Would you be more interested?

Would you be more interested if by taking a strategic approach you will, very quickly gain more persuasive power than most successful negotiators?

But I wouldn't want you to be that interested unless you are thinking about specific situations where you really want a huge amount of explosive persuasive power because next chapter we are really bringing out the big guns...

Anyway until then find a mere mortal, flap your gums at them until they get excited about life and you realise that you have totally changed in the way you are experiencing language.

Written Persuasion Patterns

Patterns Have A Great Place In
Written Form When Used With Care

A question I am being asked a lot is do NLP Language Patterns work in written form and in particular on websites and emails?

And the short answer is yes they do…

A big area of NLP is all about how we use language from a hypnotic perspective. If you are already a practitioner or master practitioner you might have had the experience of learning all the jargons, forms and patterns and not really knowing how to put it together in a meaningful way.

The Four Keys to Language Patterns

There are four key secrets to making language patterns work. The first is having a clear outcome in mind. The second is about understanding the sequence of internal representations you want your subject to go through and the third[1] is having a process to take them through. I

---

[1] Okay, so there were only 3 keys… Learn more when you read all about 'anticipation loops' ☺

know this sounds a bit woolly but it is fairly straight forward once you have some examples to work through.

With this in mind, below is an email I sent out to my list of subscribers about a language pattern course. As part of the email I offered a free place on the course for the person that did the best linguistic analysis of the email. The winner's response is also below.

John's analysis is exceptionally good and he got about 80% of the patterns and processes that I used. He got most of the rest on the course, but I am keeping a few secrets for the master class.

If you have studied NLP have a read through the original email and see if you spot as much as John. If you haven't studied NLP before go straight to John's analysis and check out how much you can do with persuasive language. It may not all make sense if you don't know the jargon but any good NLP Practitioner will be able to take you through the little bits of jargon involved. And remember whilst these patterns are more effective and usable when speaking they have a great place in written form when used with care.

Sent: 14 March 2007 16:40

Subject: Free NLP Language Development - A Beginner's Guide to Advanced Language Patterns

Hi All,

Several times recently a number of you have mentioned that *you would like to be better at persuasive language techniques*. The problem we face is that to get really good results means *you need to go beyond NLP material,* start thinking of language in terms of a process rather than the content of individual patterns and be prepared to practice in real environments. Whilst my practitioner course now goes a step further towards a solution there is much more that could be added. So, here's a course for you along with two opportunities to go for free.

A Beginner's Guide to Advanced Language Patterns

A weekend of fun and learning specifically around patterns of persuasion which will include:

- Covertly installing and/or destroying beliefs, ideas and thinking processes. Not only controlling a person's thoughts but how they are thinking them as well.

- How to lock a person's heart, body and soul into your product, service...or just into you. At the extreme, how to create cults and stalkers.

- A future pace that is so powerful that the person will not be able to stop thinking about whatever you have put into their head.

- A conversation management process that means you are more persuasive without having to think about it.

There is a lot more detail about specifically what *you will get on this course* in the attachment. You will also find some stuff about your applications, based on the course material if you can't already *imagine 1001 uses for dangerously hypnotic and persuasive language.*

As you can see from the brief points above <u>this is very serious and powerful material</u>. I know of only one other trainer in the world that is prepared to share this sort of material (Kenrick Cleveland.) Some of what I will be delivering is added refinements and developments from his material.

Because these tools are so powerful, they can do much harm or great good, depending on the intent of the user. There is too much content to deliver for us to get bogged down in discussions of ethics, morality or definitions of manipulation during the workshop so you will be asked to sign up to a code of ethics before *you attend this course.* If you are uncomfortable about having this much <u>persuasive power</u> please don't *sign up for the weekend.* If, however you have a desire to properly unlock your linguistic powers then have a read of the attachment before you make your decision.

As always I am really only interested in those who are creative, ambitious and really want to improve your skills. And I only want to supply courses that give you a <u>great return on investment</u>. So spend a few minutes thinking about the areas in your life where you want more influence. Work out what would be happening if you had this power and then how much value have you attached to getting there.

By now, you may already be understanding that this is going to be an expensive course. The fact of the matter is there is not another NLP trainer in the UK that has the skills, knowledge or courage to deliver this material. It is an area that I have studied and practiced for a whole number of years at some personal cost to me and those around me (Joe, Dave, Hope the nightmares have stopped now, and you are thinking about attending so you know he mechanics of what I was doing). And this is a whole two days of sharing that information with people that have enough foundation knowledge in place to understand it.

Have a look at what Kenrick would charge you just for his home study course and know that when I take this course to market properly I will be selling it at no less than £500. But, because this is the first one, I want to play to my home crowd and I know I can tap you for a good testimonial I have a good, one time only offer for this course. Also being aware that several of you are considering the Master Prac with me I will refund the whole price of this course if you book on my next Master Prac.

Finally, the second opportunity to come on the course for free. As you will have already recognised this email is packed full of a variety of patterns. The person that emails me the best linguistic analysis of this email will get to go on the course for free. (As a hint: there is a lot more than a few double spaced or bolded embedded commands and you will really need to start thinking about process, structure and sequences of internal representations).

Cheers

Hypnotic Language Analysis of Direct Response Email

The Winner – John Middleton's analysis of my email. John's comments are highlighted in [square brackets].

Hi All,

Several times recently a number of you have mentioned that *you would like to be better at persuasive language techniques.* [This is an embedded command to install a desire to be better] The problem we face is that to get really good results means *you need to go beyond NLP material* [a suggestion that this course will give you something beyond NLP and by suggestion that it is therefore better than NLP and standard NLP courses. There is also the suggestion that course will give you really good results], start thinking of language in terms of a process rather than the content of individual patterns and be prepared to practice in real environments. [Embedded command to start thinking about language in a new way and also a pre frame to ensure that the reader knows there will be work needed to get really good. The use of the word real suggests again a higher level than the standard NLP course - this is Big Boys stuff] Whilst my practitioner course now goes a step further towards a solution there is much more that could be added. So, here's a course for you along with two opportunities to go for free. [An anticipation loop - everyone likes anything for free - it ensures that the reader will read the entire email and it may also capture some casual readers]

A Beginner's Guide to Advanced Language Patterns

A weekend of fun and learning specifically around patterns of persuasion which will include:

- Covertly installing and/or destroying beliefs, ideas and thinking processes. Not only controlling a person's thoughts but how they are thinking them as well.

- How to lock a person's heart, body and soul into your product, service...or just into you. At the extreme, how to create cults and stalkers.

- A future pace that is so powerful that the person will not be able to stop thinking about whatever you have put into their head.

- A conversation management process that means you are more persuasive without having to think about it.

[This paragraph is all about progression and by inference mastery. From Beginner to Advanced. There is a frame suggesting that it will be fun. Each of the bullet point lines start with a normal statement that is then revved up to extremes instilling emotions of excitement and fascination in the reader. You have presented scenarios for the reader to take and make their own - something you command them to do in the last lines of the next paragraph.]

There is a lot more detail about specifically what *you will get on this course* [embedded command to get on the course] in the attachment. You will also find some stuff about your applications, based on the course material if you can't already *imagine 1001 uses for dangerously hypnotic and persuasive language.*

[The rest of this paragraph builds on the bullet points of the last paragraph getting the reader to find his own reasons to get excited about the course. The use of words such as "dangerous" suggests that course is the real thing and builds upon the real world theme from the first paragraph.]

As you can see from the brief points above <u>this is very serious and powerful material.</u> I know of only one other trainer in the world that is prepared to share this sort of material (Kenrick Cleveland, www.maxpersuasion.com). Some of what I will be delivering is added refinements and developments from his material.

[In this paragraph you continue on the powerful and dangerous theme and tie yourself in to the most prominent persuasion master (Cleveland) in the world. You then suggest that you are better than him - basically in this paragraph you have taken care of the competition.]

Because these tools are so powerful, they can do much harm or great good, depending on the intent of the user. There is too much content to deliver for us to get bogged down in discussions of ethics, morality or definitions of manipulation during the workshop so you will be asked to sign up to a code of ethics before *you attend this course.* [embedded command] If you are uncomfortable about having this much <u>persuasive power</u> please don't *sign up for the weekend.* [embedded command] If, however you have a desire to properly unlock your linguistic powers then have a read of the attachment before you make your decision. [2 embedded commands here instructing the reader to desire and then act on that desire. Again the dangerous and powerful theme is continued here keeping up the excitement that has been created in previous lines.]

As always I am really only interested in those who are creative, ambitious and really want to improve your skills. And I only want to supply courses that give you a <u>great return on investment.</u> So spend a few minutes thinking about the areas in your life where *you want more influence.* Work out what would be happening if you had this power and then how much value have you attached to getting there.

[In this paragraph you make the reader feel chosen and therefore elite. You also use a Cialdini pattern of giving something back - caring for the reader enough to want to give him something back - this is deliberately left blank to allow the reader to fill it in for himself but he has already been conditioned to do this in the last few paragraphs re the bullet points and the 1001 uses for hypnosis. You also have an embedded command there - I suspect that your intention was to make the reader feel even more of an elite by managing to make it on the course but there is also a link back to the idea that he will have to work to get these skills and that he will value the journey involved in that. You also have an embedded command in the paragraph instructing the reader to feel the need to have more influence. You also tell the reader to think of areas where this can help him - he will already be doing this it is merely an explicit command carried over from the last few paragraphs.]

By now, [embedded command] you may already be understanding that this is going to be an expensive course. The fact of the matter is there is not another NLP trainer in the UK that has the skills, knowledge or courage to deliver this material. It is an area that I have studied and practiced for a whole number of years at some personal cost to me and those around me (Joe, Dave, Hope the nightmares have stopped now, and you are thinking about attending so you know he mechanics of what I was doing). And this is a whole two days of sharing that information with people that have enough foundation knowledge in place to understand it.

[You are instructing the reader to buy the product/course and managing his expectations about price. You are emphasising the cost to you and the fact that it is a special and therefore worth it by making it unique and again there is a hint of danger. Again there is a feeling that you need to be skilled to some extent to do this course. There is also deliberate targeting of 2 people in particular

- this does 2 things - it appeals to the two people targeted giving them an embedded command that they will recognise and find humorous but will still work and it also convinces other readers that these people have been affected by these skills that you will be teaching and that they actually work. There is some history here and history makes things seem more real.]

Have a look at what Kenrick would charge you just for his home study course and know that when I take this course to market properly I will be selling it at no less than £500. But, because this is the first one, I want to play to my home crowd and I know I can tap you for a good testimonial I have a good, one time only offer for this course. Also being aware that several of you are considering the Master Prac with me I will refund the whole price of this course if you book on my next Master Prac.

[Carrying on with the Cleveland theme here and inferring that you are better than him. You are also in effect telling the reader that he is special - that you have chosen him and are linking in the benefits of attending your master prac by adding value for the reader. You are offering what in Direct Sales would be a "PS..." offer here - something for free if one takes up another opportunity that you are offering.]

Finally, the second opportunity to come on the course for free. As you will have already recognised this email is packed full of a variety of patterns. The person that emails me the best linguistic analysis of this email will get to go on the course for free. (As a hint: there is a lot more than a few double spaced or bolded embedded commands and you will really need to start thinking about process, structure and sequences of internal representations).

[In this last paragraph you are hinting at what is in the rest of the email and making the casual reader who has got this far aware that there is more here than just simple language. The chance to go for free is something that most people cannot resist. You've also shut the loop that you started in the first paragraph.]

[This email essentially opens a number of loops, gives the reader benefit statements, commands him/her to find their own reasons to go on the course, provides them with commands and reasons to get excited and commands them to think how they would apply these skills. Most readers having read this will have felt excitement and imagined the power that going on this course and learning these skills (and you make it quite clear that it will be hard work) will give them. There is also the sense that they will be going beyond simple NLP and in to areas that only the elite know about!!!]

As you can imagine it was a very powerful and exciting course for both the delegates and myself. John got his free place and was surprised at how much of the email he had missed. Feel free to pick up any more and email me the extra bits that you spot. I will publish any good responses.

And no, I am not running this course anymore.

The Difference Between Written and Spoken Patterns

There are differences between spoken and written patterns. Spoken patterns are intangible and can therefore be far less subtle, but everything we have studied together works in written form and you will see my website and emails littered with this material all the time. The key focus for written patterns is looking at a strategic sequence of internal representations rather than a focus on specific patterns.

Putting It All Together

Why Use One Pattern When You Can Develop Whole Sequences To Fire Off Together?

When I first started learning about hypnotic persuasion I took a few patterns every day and just spoke them at someone. Every day it would be a new pattern, I didn't care who or what the situation was I would just make a point of blurting out a pattern and then got really proud of myself for having had a go, whilst leaving some highly confused innocent standing in my wake wondering why I was speaking so strangely.

The truth about these patterns is that no single pattern is going to automatically give you the result you want. Having a process and a sequence of patterns that guide the subject towards your outcomes is what will make this work. In this section we are going to start putting together all the pieces so that you can put sequences of patterns together in a coherent way.

The outcome of this lesson is for you to be able to construct influencing scripts, sequences and processes that lead people to where you want to go.

Covert Hypnotic Influencing Scripts To Accelerate Your Progress

This lesson we are going to focus on putting all of these patterns together in to a few paragraphs and scripts so that in the next section we can turn them into conversations. The idea being that I am going to train you to think more strategically about persuasion and how you are going to influence the outcome directly without having to be concerned about specific language patterns.

Hypnotic Persuasion Scripts

At this point some people complain that they don't see the relevance of scripts and that they would prefer to be in the flow of a conversation rather than spewing large amounts of language at someone.

If you said that I would almost agree with you.

The issue is not about memorising large scripts, but is all about learning how persuasive language works, building a library of useful phrases in your head and practicing fitting patterns into a real context. By taking this approach you will very quickly learn how to integrate patterns, make them a natural part of your language and also start to think strategically about how you apply sequences of patterns.

Here is an example of strategic thinking in terms of persuasion skills from a graduate of my NLP practitioner course. Here is that process deconstructed.

NLP Practitioner Graduate 2005, John McKinstry

John McKinstry graduated from his NLP Practitioner Course a few years ago and is regularly practicing and applying NLP Techniques. Recently he has been having some trouble with his mobile phone leading to several calls with the airtime provider and even a visit to one of their shops. Each of these contacts proved fruitless, annoying and were getting John increasingly angry about the situation. He then took the situation in hand and got a great result. This is his story and I will apply some comments about specific NLP Techniques and concepts at the end.

After several horrendous experiences with the airtime provider I knew I wasn't getting anywhere other than more angry. I decided I would give their call centre one last chance to put it right.

Firstly I made sure that I knew what I wanted as a result. This was quite easy as it is fairly straightforward, I wanted my phone fixed. The next thing I did was let go of all my anger so I could speak calmly, professionally and with persuasion. Before I made the call I made sure that I knew the patterns that I was going to apply.

When I got through to the call centre the first thing I said to the agent was something like "At the moment you have a very angry customer on the line who may well want to cancel your service because of what I have been through. How would you like to make that customer a very happy man and willing to sing the praises of your company?"

The agent's response was "of course I would" and I responded, "great then all you need to do is..." I explained clearly and succinctly what I needed. From there this call centre agent moved heaven and earth to give me what I wanted. The service was so good that I later spoke to the agent's manager to praise him and he later got a quality service award.

This is a brilliant example of how persuasion skills should work and here are a few points that are worthy of note.

State Control & NLP Persuasion Skills

Most people would recognize that when they are angry that their skills diminish. The reason behind this is that your brain will have activated a fight or flight response. This inhibits your creativity, your spontaneity and restricts your options to either fight or flight. For persuasion skills to work well you need to be in a position where you have the most flexibility, the most creativity and the ability to react in any given direction. John did exactly the right thing by letting go of the anger before dealing with the problem.

Planning for Hypnotic Persuasion Techniques

The pre-planning that John went through is excellent. It he started off by working out exactly what he wanted. One of the key issues in persuasion skills is a persuasion engineer not really knowing what they want as an outcome. Although not explicit in John's comments simply by his actions I know he took this next, very vital step. He considered the benefits to the other person for doing what he wanted.

NLP Hypnotic Persuasion Patterns

The pattern John used is a very elegant version of the first pattern you learnt in this book. The pattern, called a redefine, can be described simply as:

"the issue isn't (x); it's (y) and would you like to fix it?"

John led the agent into the current situation; he then explained how the situation could be changed (covertly giving the agent the benefits as well). John then asked the question, "Would you prefer that?" This is a presuppositional question and the concept is fully explored in a previous chapter. For the moment it is fairly obvious that the answer to this question can only really be "yes" and that it starts sealing the commitment of the agent.

John then explains explicitly what the agent has to do to achieve this result. Although John doesn't state above that he ends his description with another question I would hope he said something like "are you prepared to help me do this?" This is another presuppositional question and if answered with a yes would seal the commitment of the agent even further.

Deconstructing this little piece of NLP persuasion language in the real world is an excellent opportunity to see how persuasion skills should work. Both parties got a terrific win-win result. An observation though is that John would not have got this result without the planning he put in and the reality of this is not about the patterns but about setting in motion a sequence of events that funnels everything towards your result.

Hypnotic Persuasion, More Than Just a Language Pattern

We have focused just on the linguistic elements of this example. You might want to bear in mind that a good NLP practitioner course will show you how to let go of negative emotions, think in terms of process as well as building rapport face to face and over the phone instantly. All of these things had bearing on John's situation.

This should be enough for you to recognise the value of spending a few minutes planning for persuasion. The easiest way of developing this skill is by creating, writing and speaking some scripts out loud. This forces you to think in a persuasive way and the ability becomes more instinctive.

A Strategic Approach Example

I want you to start thinking about the sequence of internal representation you are taking your subject through…

Let us say you are writing a sales script for a personal development course. Bombarding your prospect with huge benefit statements might not have the desired effect. Here is a possible sequence I might want a prospect to go through:

1. Mild interest/anticipation.

2. Recognising their needs.

3. Establishing the benefits of filling those needs, including future pacing in to bigger benefits.

4. Excitement at filling those needs.

Please note for the sales professionals amongst you, this is not a sales process as such, just a way of thinking about the emotional journey your prospect is going through.

Now filling in a little more detail, the conversation might look more like this:

1. One line story about a person getting an incredible result (just the result, not how they achieved it), ending in "what would you like to achieve" statements.

2. Presuppositional questions about what is stopping them achieving and the implications of staying down the same path.

3. Future paced statements about having the tools to do it differently, how things get better now and even better in the future.

4. Attach all those feelings to presenting the product.

Let me now develop the script further so you have a complete worked example:

1. *Have you met Ethel? She is just off to hop round the Sahara Dessert backwards, is being sponsored by Pepsi for millions to do it and fulfilling a life long ambition. Amazing really because last week she was working as an excess navel fluff remover with no prospects. All she needed was a small switch in the way she was thinking to then go chasing her dreams.*

2. *Wouldn't it be amazing if you could go chasing your dreams? If you could, what dreams would you chase? What is important to you to about going for* [insert their answers]*? I don't know if you have done this, but did you have all those plans, dreams and ambitions when you were younger and then as you*

grow up daily life gets in the way of getting the things that you want. What stops you from going after your dreams? [At this point you could really ramp up the bad feelings, you know the sort of thing, what a loss, getting to the end of your life with unfulfilled ambitions, imagine laying in your deathbed thinking of all those might have beens etc. But play this carefully, I personally prefer having happy thoughts rather than sad ones so don't normally go far down this line.]

3. *The thing about Ethel though was just a small shift in her thinking let her get going; doing all the things that she has always wanted to and never knew how. Incredibly she let go of all your fear and past failures. You can change your beliefs, become more self confident and motivated to getting all the things you want.* [Notice the switch from Ethel to you... looks obvious here, but your prospect will not see it]. *How good would you feel if you can let go of your past and embrace the future in a way that you can get the things you want?* [Ramp this up as much as you like. Probably the best way to go would be to ask questions... how would you feel, what would you be seeing, doing saying next year, two years later etc.]

4. The issue is not about Ethel getting these results but whether you can learn to do the same for yourself. Would you like me to show you the course where Ethel learned how to run her mind in such a way that you can achieve all those things we have been talking about?

If you haven't guessed already Ethel is fake… but the course isn't. It is all about *NLP and Self Hypnosis for Fun and Profit*. This is still not a sales script, just an emotional journey for your prospect and some ideas for how some of the language fits in.

You could make this a lot more advanced by now thinking about objections and where they will occur, if you already know the prospect integrating their language and interests and so on.

But we will leave it here so you get an opportunity to go through a few thought processes and practice some scripting for yourself. Remember the objective here is getting to think in terms of sequences of internal representations and how your persuasive language fits into all of that.

NLP Sales Process, Deconstructed

An NLP Strategic Approach to Sales Persuasion

Here is a version of my sales process with some of the elements of NLP deconstructed. I hope by reading through this you can get some ideas of your own and it demonstrates where and how elements of NLP can be integrated into a sales process and gives you another way of thinking your way through a Strategic Persuasion Process.

Before Meeting The Prospect

- Make sure I am in the right frame of mind.

- Use 'perceptual positions' to get into the mindset of the prospect and understand how they are thinking. Do I know my product from the prospect's perspective? For example:

  o What problem/need does it address?

  o What can they expect as results?

  o How do I have to articulate these benefits for it to be meaningful for them?

Initial Part of Meeting

- Building trust, rapport and setting the scene.

- Clarifying the outcomes for this meeting.

- Delivering a hook or incentive for the buyer to want to be involved in the process i.e. why should they bother listening to me?

- Opening anticipation loops, setting expectations, laying the foundations of any covert hypnotic elements I am thinking of using.

Needs Analysis

Asking questions to find out what the prospect needs and understanding how they represent the world to themselves. Good questions are obviously based on the context you are in, but here are some that I ask based on the context of selling personal development courses:

- What do you see yourself doing in five years time?

- How confident are you in achieving this?

- What skills, beliefs, and mindset would you have to take on to make this easier to achieve?

- What happens if you don't achieve these things?

- What does gaining these things give you?

- What is important to you about achieving these things?

- What value would you put on having the beliefs, mindset and skills to achieve your goals?

Notice the sequence of these questions and what is presupposed in the answers. They are specifically in this order so the prospect is going from identifying their need, to the consequences of meeting and not meeting these needs and finally attaching a value to the need.

If they don't have a need or don't attach a value that is greater than my price for the solution then I have to walk away because they cannot be a customer of mine.

Linking Solutions to Needs

Once my prospect is in touch with their need and they recognise a value to meeting this need I am going to present them with my course as a solution. When you study NLP this can seem quite complicated, for example many NLPers will start talking about hypnotic language patterns, anchoring positive emotions to your product and negative states to the competition, and the covert use of a hundred different NLP techniques.

Personally I believe if you ask questions in a meaningful sequence and present your solutions in a meaningful way then you can keep things simple and get the business.

This doesn't stop me using hypnotic language patterns and non-verbal NLP techniques, but my experience has shown if I get the basic foundations right all of this is icing on the cake. If I get the basics wrong all the advanced NLP Techniques at my disposal have never saved the situation.

Handling The Objections

Normally with any complex product, service or sales negotiation there are details that need to be ironed out. As such I expect my prospects to question, query and challenge me over the product, the process or what value it is for them.

Often sales people get themselves into trouble here because they take the challenges personally and as a sign the prospect is not interested or not going to buy. Oddly objections only come up if they are interested in the product. Think about this from your own experience. Consider a telephone sales call when you are busy, distracted and generally not wanting to talk to a stranger, but you pick the phone up just in case it is important.

If you are not interested in the product or service do you not just try and get them off the phone as quickly as possible?

Alternatively imagine that in the first few seconds the sales person mentions something you have been thinking of buying. The chances are you will either speak with them or arrange another time to call.

The secret to handling objections is to recognise them as buying signals and deal with them accordingly.

Asking For The Business

I separate this bit out because it can be problematic. Some sales people have a fear of rejection or don't believe in the product just as we discussed above. This sometimes has the consequences of them never getting round to asking for the business. If you have dealt with the issue as discussed above this problem won't occur.

Often following this process the prospect will lead the situation and tell you they have heard enough and just want to buy. This is a great situation because all you have to do is stop talking and take the money.

The usual circumstances are that you have to ask the prospect if they are ready to buy now. If they are then take the money. If they are not then you are going back to the objection phase and uncovering what is stopping them.

Even when people are ready to buy they sometimes need the prompt of you asking for the business before they are prepared to hand over the money. This is quite normal and is only about needing a little push to complete the decision.

Stopping Buyer's Remorse

The final part of the sales process is often forgotten despite having huge importance. Have you ever bought something and then regretted it? Part of a sales professional's duty is to make sure they are fully happy with the product now, when they get it home... and for the lifetime of the product.

There are many ways of doing this but my favoured approach is an NLP technique which is called a Hypnotic Future Pace. In simple terms I will get the customer to imagine themselves using the product, getting everything they want from it, and generally enjoying themselves having made a great decision. As I am doing this I am checking for anything that might come up as an objection and dealing with it.

A typical example in my context might be people thinking that after they have been on a course that they forget how to use a particular skill or process. So whilst I am getting them to see themselves in the future and they express this fear I tell them about the comprehensive manual, the groups of graduates that support each other and the opportunities to retake the course for free.

I then take them into enjoying the results they are getting from having completed a great course where they have learned all the things that you need to get the results you are after. By using language in a specific way you can get your customers to experience having used the product and if everything has been dealt with this will reassure them that they have made the right decision.

If you need any more examples of this approach just have a look through my website and you will find lots of places where I have taken exactly this approach… in fact you could chart the sequences of internal representations as an exercise in itself.

Next lesson we will start to look at how you can, armed with this information, turn it into a conversation and even better won't have to remember patterns, scripts or even your own name if you don't want to.

Using Comparisons to Accelerate a State

How Would You Get People Excited By Asking A Question... Would This Be A Skill Worth Knowing?

Sharon came up with the idea of asking the difference between two states so your subject has to try on each to find the difference between the two:

"What is the difference between boredom and excitement?"

This almost works.

The one thing you might want to consider is that by using two wildly different states the comparison is too easy. If you were to use two very *close* states however, the subject has to go through both and really examine the difference:

"What is the difference between being interested and curiosity?"

Or if you were to ramp it up a little:

"What's the difference between being totally engrossed and insatiably curious?"

I'll show you some patterns using comparisons and anticipation loops later if you can tell me the difference between being wildly excited about the idea and having a burning desire to just know more.

Decision Destroying Patterns

John brought up the idea of using tenses in much the same way as we have been talking about emotions and states. This works in exactly the same way and can be very effective, for example.

When someone has made a decision that you don't like you might reply with:

"Where were you when you are deciding that?"

This question is deliberately putting the subject back in the past when they made a 'decision' (sounds fixed in time) and then moving it into the present and turning it back to the process of 'deciding'. From this point whatever they say you have a range of options to start moving them towards what you want. Here are two of them:

1. *"The issue is not how you were deciding in the past but how we can work together to get you (insert massive benefits from deciding in your favour)..."*

2. *"That's right you were (insert their answer to the previous question) and now what do we have to say or do to get (insert those massive benefits again)..."*

NLP Language: Future Pacing & Thought Binds

Another thought around the same ideas came from Dave about extending things out to the future. Imagine what it would be like if, every time you turned on a light switch, you just suddenly thought of three new language patterns. How many new patterns would you have by the end of the week? Now the quantity and quality of those patterns are not the issue. But how confident, excited and just on top of this game would you be? I'm not going to say this is what is happening, but consider a couple of weeks time when you have done this and realised that reading through this paragraph, imagining this happening was the start of the process. How good does that make you feel?

Okay, I'm not going to say any more about thought binds, every thing you need is in the above paragraph. Read it through a couple of times, spot the changes in tenses, notice the anchor to a common action, feel good about the emotional shifts and then write out ten of your own for sets of circumstance you might find yourself in. Here are some ideas to start you off.

NETWORKING

It has been a pleasure talking to you. I have a feeling we will want to get in contact soon. I don't know if that will be next month, next week or in a couple of days. But when you are feeling good about the conversation we had and how we might progress our business together in the future you will find my number on this card [obviously handing over your business card at this point]. *Wouldn't it be good if by the end of the year you are successfully getting more* [insert massive benefits that they are after] *and it all started from just looking for the number on this card?*

118

DATING

Some people like to go for the direct approach. I think you want a slow, but passionate response that just builds more and more excitement until you can't help but act on impulse. As a hopeless romantic imagine what it is like when you start to think of someone and you just know they are stuck in your mind, last thing you think of before falling asleep, first think you think of when you wake and each time the thought comes it builds more excitement, more energy until you just have to give in to your desires. Now that is something worth waiting for don't you think? [If everything has gone well up to this point, make an excuse and leave, they will be chasing after you.]

TRAINING WITH LANGUAGE PATTERNS

Let's start from the results you are after from this course. What will you be able to do, what do you want to achieve, and what goals do you have as a result of successfully finishing this course? When you have thought of what the end result looks like project out in to the future, what will you be like next week, next month, next year? As you get a sense of that jot a few words down or draw a little picture on these post it notes. [Once they have done this put the post it notes on the walls.]

As you get a few moments through the day have a look at some of the post it notes and talk to each other about your expectations, as you do this you will notice that your own goals seem easier to achieve and more concrete. The reason this is happening is because as we go through the course and you are keeping your expectations alive in this way you will feed all the course content into your direct applications and realise how you can achieve even more... Strange how this can happen just through putting up a few post it notes on the walls. How much stranger will it feel when next week as you are using these skills in work you suddenly look back towards now and realised that is exactly what is happening... now the first subject we will be talking about is....

HYPNOTIC LANGUAGE IN SALES

I only want you to buy because you have realised this product is the right one for you. The way to understand that it is right for you is to look out to the future to next week and find yourself having fun, getting results and [insert massive benefits] directly through using this product. Every time you look at this product I want you to break out into a smile because you are imagining all the benefits you are getting from it. When you are doing that, not now, but imagining you are doing it in the future then you already know this is exactly the right thing for you.

That should give you a few ideas to pick and choose from. Now go and create a few paragraphs for yourself in your own contexts. Email them in and I will publish the best of them on the website.

Moving from Monologues to Hypnotic Persuasive Conversations

Persuasion is Not About a One-Way Scripted Monologue, But a Two Way Process That Engages Both Parties

Now we are going to take all those scripts and turn them in to conversations. Active participation by the other party is the key. Often you will find just implanting a seed of a direction in a person's head is all you need for them to get the whole idea and do what you want.

As an overall pattern if you look for the benefit your subject gains from complying with your wishes and then you present that in a meaningful way to them it is a complete win/win situation. Taking this approach the best influence and persuasion you can have with people is not about leading them to water but just pointing them in the right direction. This means that persuasion is not about a one-way scripted monologue, but a two way process that engages both parties. Now we are going to explore how you can use some of the processes and patterns we have learned to create exactly that conversation.

How To Become More Conversational With Hypnotic Persuasion

Before we start properly here are a couple of ideas that have already been stated but are so important that they are worth stating again.

NLP Technique: Perceptual Positions

If I can plan before hand for my persuasion encounter one of the things I will do is a Perceptual Positions exercise. I will imagine myself as my subject whether it is a group, individual or organisation. Obviously the better I know them the easier and more accurate this will be, but I will do it even when I have no clue about the person involved. The reason being is that it sets my unconscious mind to trying to think the way they do. I am looking to understand their beliefs, values, problems and benefits in the context of what I want them to do as well as generally matching their verbal and non-verbal language. All of this will help me greatly in a persuasion context. Basically I am building rapport even before I have met them.

NLP Language: Pattern Delivery

I have said this before and I think it is so important that it bears saying again. Most people speak too fast and too high for real persuasion to work. Think, Barry White and you will have the idea. Also having the flexibility to slow right down, speed up, take your voice higher or lower makes a huge difference. All of these things are easily learnt... ten minutes a day in front of the mirror saying your patterns and you will have it within a week.

As a general note starting slowly and speeding up give the impression of gaining energy or excitement. Going from fast to slow draws the energy out and can make people withdraw into themselves and is a great trance inducer. Anyway onwards towards the lesson...

Let us now move on to conversation management.

Hypnotic Persuasive Conversations

So far we have really been looking at scripts and monologues. Conversations are not really like this as we have to give the other person an opportunity to speak and we have to connect what they say to what we are saying. On top of this we are now thinking on another level and you are noticing the sequences of internal representations, the emotional journey and looking for specific outcomes. Sounds like a tall order?

Let me start with the general process for a conversation. If you are managing the conversation, and if you are in a persuasion situation you should be managing the conversation, a good overall process would be:

1. **Inform** – Make a statement

2. **Invite** – Ask for a response

3. **Acknowledge** – make sure that the other party knows you were listening to them

Here is a typical, making small talk at a party example:

- **Inform** – *"John always throws great parties."*

- **Invite** – *"How do you know him?"*

- **Acknowledge** – *"You know him from work."*

- **Inform** – *"From what John says it seem a great place to work."*

- **Invite** – *"What do you do there?"*

- **Acknowledge/Inform/Invite** – *"Interesting job, how did you get to be doing that?"*

And so on. You might be thinking to yourself that this is a typical type of conversation and why am I making such a big deal about deconstructing the process. The answer is that by taking apart the process of conversing you now have a way of fitting various parts of a script into the conversation whilst keeping the flow. Let's look at this conversation again but add in a few random state changes and patterns.

NLP Seduction Script... A Beginning

Inform:

> *"I always get a great feeling about being invited to one of John's parties because I know you get to meet such interesting people."*

This is so sneaky, seems like an off-hand compliment, but notice I have shifted the 'I' to a 'You' and if you are studying the non verbal elements here is where you would start anchoring stuff to yourself. Some of you have been spotting the embedded commands that appear occasionally in my language. For those of you that aren't spotting them yet some of them are <u>underlined</u> through this conversation.

Invite:

> *"How do you know John?"*

Acknowledge:

> *"From what he says it must be a great place to work."*

Inform:

> *"It seems like a place full of lively and exciting people. I am really interested in places where <u>you can get excited and passionate</u> about what you do."*

Invite:

> *"What is it about what you do that you can get really passionate about?"*

Acknowledge:

> *"Wow, I didn't realise how exciting filing can be."*

Inform:

"I was reading somewhere that passion like any other emotional state takes time to <u>build to a peak. With me</u> it is a slow burn. I first see something [if I have good rapport here I will replace something with someone] *I think I am going to enjoy, I start thinking of the things that I find interesting about it/them and the feeling just starts in my stomach and just moves up getting more and more intense, until you <u>just have to act on impulse</u>."*

Invite:

> *"How do you experience it?"*

Acknowledge/Inform/Invite:

"Your toes start to curl... I can imagine that. I wonder if different emotions have different feelings. What is the difference between passion and total desire for you?"

And so on...

Don't get too excited about this just yet. Let me explain what you have here first. In real simple terms, when you put some of the ideas about scripting together with this conversation management approach you now have a way of automatically steering the conversation in any way you want it to go. All you have to do is acknowledge the elements of the conversation that are heading the right way and use them to build the next frame.

This is powerful stuff and the first time I have ever deconstructed the process in writing. Treat it with the love, care and attention it deserves and it will serve you well.

So now we need to talk about how you are going to practice this and start integrating it into all of your conversations. The first thing I would suggest is to let go of everything except the process.

Use the Inform, Invite, Acknowledge process to just guide a conversation. Spot how this happens naturally and then just start tinkering with it. Within a few days as you get more familiar with it gently start adding a few patterns and notice the reactions you are getting, if they are going the right way start accelerating them, if they are not going the right way switch directions.

Let go of any expectations except to see what will happen. The idea is that you are playing and practicing. As you start to build a library of patterns and phrases you will automatically find yourself going in to this mode and guiding conversations in the direction you want.

The next chapter is the end. The end of the beginning, there is much we have not yet covered and many new things to learn. We will talk about next steps and how you can keep your progress accelerating. We will talk about how you can use this sort of thinking to blow out your own issues. We will end with some more examples, scripts and applications and set you up for the future.

In the mean time find some mere mortals, listen to them flap their gums at you and gently steer them to a better way of life than they have ever experienced before.

Persuading a Disillusioned Team
A Process Deconstructed

Here is another script and analysis of the process. A couple of you have emailed in with particular scenarios. Here is my construction based on some of your personal situations.

NLP Leadership: Team Management

The situation I am thinking about is where I have to get my team to implement changes that they won't like and see no benefit to… and I agree with them.

My thought process starts with what is the benefit to me/the team for implementing these changes… and I am going to hold to the only real benefit is that we won't lose our jobs if we implement the changes.

The sequence of events I might plan out might go something like (including the expected emotional journey):

1. Set some frames/expectations [wary, hesitant]

2. Announce the change [anger/frustration]

3. Uncover benefits [begrudging agreement]

4. Build team identity [sense of cohesion, support and identity]

5. Negotiate roles/tasks [more motivated]

6. Seal commitment/future pace [feeling better about the situation]

Now let's add some more flesh to these bones:

1. *I have some announcements to make and we have some decisions to take. They are not as bad as the company going bankrupt and us all being unemployed, but you won't like them. Unfortunately we have no choice in this so we just have to deal with it.* [Notice the anticipation loop and the use of very negative internal representations here (bankrupt... unemployed) I want the team to think the worst so they can breathe a sigh of relief when I actually tell them what needs to be done.]

2. *It has been decided by our Board of Directors that the company is now going to have to (x) and we have been given the task of sorting it out.* [I am deliberately deflecting the anger/frustration away from me and towards the Board here.] *This is non-negotiable, but what is negotiable is how we go about it.* [I am rolling straight from something they have no control over into something they can do deliberately to give them some sense of control. If they are a very task focused team this might be enough to pull them together.]

3. *The company is doing this because* [unveil all the reasons that it is thought good for the company], *but we know this won't be good for us. Can we spend a few minutes discussing what we might gain from this?* [Just in case I've missed

anything and it gives them more control and I would rather facilitate from them the fact that they are being paid to do this job.]

4. *A thought I have just had is that the issue is not what we have been asked to do, but the fact that as a team we perform well whether it is in our favour or not. I don't know about you guys, but I don't think I want to give the company the opportunity to say this failed because we didn't put our support into it. What would you say to just getting this done with as little time and effort as possible so no one can say we haven't given it our best shot?* [Etc. etc. I could show you how to leverage individual and team values to turn this into a rabble rousing speech... but I think you already have enough ideas.]

5. [Not much to say here, just get them to decide which bits of what they are doing. Give them choice and get them the bits they would like most if possible and make sure that they commit publicly (see Cialdini's book on influence if you need to know why).]

6. *So we have decided it will take about four weeks to get this done. I am going to write the press release for it now and put it on our notice board so we all have a focus on the end result and we can look back on today as the start of the end of this project.* [Finally I would put up the press release and make sure it details each person with the role/assignment they have agreed to.]

The End of the Beginning
More Ideas and Patterns to Play with on the Last Day of School

So we are finally at the end and I hope you have gained what you need and more than you expected. Sat, writing this I am conscious of the fact that there is so much more that I have to share. We never spoke about installing programmed thought processes, covertly changing belief systems or using metaphors (probably the sneakiest and most covert persuasion techniques ever). Since you have made it this far into the book, consider subscribing to *Advanced Persuasion Patterns* where we take all these persuasion skills and more to a completely new level.

Let me know your thoughts about the course and the results that you have been getting. I'll put them up on the website as aid, encouragement and inspiration for others going through this book.

Now we will look at some examples of conversation management and think about how to keep your progress accelerating.

The real way to make this work is to go out there and have a go. Let go of fear, doubt and expectations, but just go out and have fun throwing some patterns about. Very quickly as you relax in to doing this you will suddenly find yourself getting better and better results and wondering how this all started.

Using NLP Language Patterns in The Real World

Do you remember the last day of school summer term? The teacher would let you bring your games in and you could play all day. You would have that mixed feeling of great, school is almost over for the whole of the summer... and I am going to miss my school, my friends and my teacher.

Today this course is over, but the rest of your life is just starting. As you think back to where you started and what you now know about language have you realised just how much has changed?

I don't know how much you have practiced or have been using... but I am guessing that if all you have done is read through these patterns then your whole view of language has changed anyway. And if you have practiced, have been putting these patterns into place then some very amazing things have been happening around you.

NLP Conversation Management: Dealing with Hecklers and Street Hawkers

This was me walking through town the other day after finishing writing a chapter for this book and trying to get my Christmas shopping done. I was stopped by one of the Hari Krishna mob. I have had it in my mind for a while that it would be fun to see if I could sell them an influencing skills course.

Watch for the patterns and the conversation management process in operation. So this is the nub of the conversation...

Hari Krishna: "Can you say Garunga?"

Me: *"Yes I can, can you say Merry Christmas?"*

HK: "Uhm... Merry Christmas, can you say Garunga?"

Me: *"The issue is not whether I can say the word, but the influencing process behind it. A great place to find out more is Cialdini's book called Influence. Have you read it?"*

HK: "Err, No..."

Me: *"Well luckily for you I have a great way of finding out more about influence and persuasion tactics just like the one you are trying to use on me. Would you like to know more?"*

HK: "No thanks, I want to tell you about..."

Me: *"I understand you have some things you want to talk about and you would find it much easier with me and all the other people you speak to if you had a good understanding of influence and persuasion tactics and how they apply to you. What do I have to say or do to get you excited about finding out more?"*

HK: "I'm not sure that..."

Me: *"That's right you are not sure yet because*

> *we haven't yet discussed the benefits. Can I*
> *start telling you about..."*

At this point he starts to walk off and I follow him. Eventually we start a conversation about persuasion skills. I spectacularly failed to sell him a course, but he did give me one of his little books in an effort to get rid of me.

NLP Customer Service, Dealing with Angry Customers

This is a cut down version of a conversation Stuart, a telephone customer service agent had recently. Again the patterns and the process shine through really clearly.

Customer: "I'm really angry, I've just got (x) and it is not anything like the advert."

Stuart: *"I realise you are very angry and I would like to help. What do I have to do for you to calm down and get this issue resolved?"*

C: "Oh... I want a complete refund."

S: *"Our policy doesn't allow us to give refunds on software products, but I am sure we can come to some arrangement to make sure that you get what you need. Tell me more about what you want the software to do."*

C: "What do you mean you won't give me a refund when it doesn't do what I want it to do?"

S: *"I realise that it is not doing what you want, and that we don't give refunds on software, but I can help by getting one of*

> *our engineers to talk to you about getting it working the way you want. All you need do is start by telling me more about what you are using it for and then I can get one of our engineers to talk you through how to get it working properly for you. Tell me more about what you are looking to achieve."*

C: "Well, what I was looking for was…"

Not a great situation because what the customer was looking for was not an option that could be offered, but a great job of talking the customer down and passing them on to someone that might be able to help.

NLP Seductions Patterns

This is John in fine flow sat opposite a woman he has never met before on a train. There is so much going on here I don't know where to start, but see what you notice.

John: *"I love that broach, it looks great on you. Tell me were you born with good taste or is it something you learned?"*

Woman: (giggle) "It was a present from my mother."

John: *"Great, even better I love people that have family with great taste, I'm looking for a Christmas present for my sister… do you think your mother might help me out choosing something?"*

Woman: "Hee, Hee."

John: *"I guess not then, but tell me, I am looking for something that she will just love, you know when you look at someone* [apparently he did really do the I/You and the someone/something shifts and she didn't notice] *and just melt because you have to have it. That is the sort of present I would like to get my sister, what would get you going the same way?"*

Woman: "Well, I don't know really, she will have different tastes…"

[lots of gum flapping taken out including introductions and rapport building, but ending with this great phrase below]

John: *"I know that you are different, but everyone has those deep hidden passions and desires that you can just tap in to when you are ready to do that now* [what a great embedded command] *what would do that for you?"* [This is great ambiguity here… are we discussing the sister or the woman, a present, John… who knows, and it is a great persuasive trance induction resulting in the exchange of phone numbers!]

Hypnotic Patterns: Ending The Beginning

We are at the end and I hope that it has been as much fun for you exploring this subject as it has for me writing it. We have travelled a long path together and there are many roads yet to walk. It would be a great pleasure to accompany you on some of those travels, so feel free to let me know of any great linguistic journeys you intend to take because if I can I would walk some of the way with you.

There are so many things that we have yet to cover. We have not yet properly talked about rapport, embedded commands, metaphors, opening anticipation loops, anchors, fractionation, rep systems and sub modality shifts, how to build and maintain a persuasive mind set and confidence, as well as a hundred and one other things that we could bring to persuasion skills.

And I should remind you here that I am not altruistic in all this. I am not doing this because I am a good person (although I like to think I am) and I am not doing this because I like you (although I would like to think I will like you when we meet). I am doing this so you might realise that if I can give you material like this in an inexpensive book, I must have some really powerful material kept specifically for those who pay big. If you are thinking this, then you would be right.

I hope you would consider a good NLP Practitioner Course or at least a download subscription course such as *Advanced Persuasion Patterns* as the ideal bolt on to this material. It would be a great way to develop the components around the linguistic ideas we have discussed as well as to deepen and extend the knowledge you already have.

In any case keep coming back to the website as there will be more and more published under NLP Techniques. As more people come through the courses, read this book and send me emails I will publish their results on the site as well. Feel free to join us on

Facebook at www.fbook.me/persuasion where there are some video presentations and the opportunity to interact with like minded persuasive peole.

But this is really just the start of some very big things for you if you choose it. Imagine for a moment embracing all of your persuasive potential and running headlong out into your future achieving all those great things that have been tickling at the back of your mind since you were eight years old. Think about where you would be looking back from five years time thinking things differently. This being the end of the beginning of being able to succeed at everything you have set out for yourself.

Spending just ten minutes a day speaking new patterns out loud, applying patterns to those thoughts in your head, planning sequences of internal representations will make you naturally brilliant at linguistic skills.

I am often complimented about my depth of understanding and fluency with linguistic skills and am often asked about how I developed them. The answer is in the little paragraph above with one tiny addition... having the courage to just go and deliver patterns to other people with no expectations, fear or favour. Very soon you will be getting results without trying, with language that seems natural and surprising yourself.

Now this part of your journey is over and we are parting. Hopefully our paths will cross again, but until then, this is that last day of school, you do have those games with you... so just find a partner and play for the whole summer.

Miscellaneous Patterns & Examples to Play With

Getting Your Subject To Keep Thinking About The Benefits of Doing What You Want Them To Do

Following are three examples of specific NLP language patterns in three different contexts. The first is an example of using covert hypnosis to start a training course, the second is about hypnotic seduction and the third is for networking in a business context.

Each example is about getting your subject to keep thinking about the benefits of doing what you want them to do. For those of you that are into NLP jargon this is about future pacing, anchoring the benefits and linguistically binding the subject to your outcomes.

Any good NLP Training Course (including *Advanced Persuasion Patterns*), will show you how the benefits of a 'VAdK strategy' for persuasion, how to install it and how to fire it off. You will also learn how to linguistically bind, future pace and amplify thoughts in the direction you want. That is what these examples really demonstrate in these three contexts.

I have put some notes in brackets, but there is a lot more going on than just the bits I point out.

Covert Hypnotic Scripts

I use these patterns every day, but not in the very condensed forms they are in here. These examples are written very tightly and written as a monologue. In a live environment I would be building all of these scripts into a flow through a conversation with more padding and some interaction with the subject. For example with the hypnotic seduction script it might take me 30 to 40 minutes to get through it.

Voice Pitch, Tone & Volume Again

Finally consider tone, pace and pitch as mentioned before. Advancing on your subject with a weedy, high-pitched voice running at light speed will not get them to access states, let alone future pace or bind them. Actually it might, but not in a way you would want.

A good hypnotic voice is slower than normal, deeper and gravely. Learning about charisma patterns and how to draw people in to a trance with just your pace and tone of voice would be a good thing… and you have enough material in this book to give you a great head start in that direction. So for the moment just consider delivering these phrases in a voice that is deeper and slower than normal.

Here are examples of using Hypnotic Language in written form.

Covert Hypnosis: A Training Example

At the beginning of a course:

Imagine for a moment that this was a great course and you have learnt all the things you need to. Sometime out in the future you might look back towards now and see this as the start of something great, perhaps you have [obviously you would be padding this out with some of the results they can expect perhaps stretching this to the extreme if it is the right sort of course and you are that sort of trainer].

When I think back on some of the course that I have been on that have given you great results [notice the switch in referential index], *I invite you to notice how much you have changed by taking on board these key concepts* [notice the switch in tense]. *Key concepts like...* [List the key ideas from your course].

You might not understand how these concepts can be used right now, but suppose for a moment you can see yourself [list more benefits from the course in the present tense], *logically you might get a sense of the good feelings you will have. Now, I don't want you to think of these results as something that happens magically just because you are focused, keen and getting involved in this course. I want you to realise that it will happen only because you have already started the process of imagining how you are using the material.* [There is so much going on in this paragraph that I wouldn't know where to begin to explain it. Call my office for the analysis if you are really that curious about it].

So, this is not a course in trying to learn (x), but just doing (y) and the more you do the more (x) will happen naturally. Anyway, if you can see the results you want, have understood the benefits for you perhaps you can already get excited about moving on to the first session [more binds and layering in a VAdK strategy].

But, just before we start can I get you to open your work books. You can obviously see some sense in keeping notes on all the bits that feel right for you [there is the VAdK strategy again]. *So can we start that process now by listing all the benefits you will get from this course on page 4* [give them some time to get their personal objectives, perhaps even discuss it with each other and if you want to go for the bolts and braces approach group tasks around this until they have one flip chart that has all their personal stake in the course written on it].

We will put the flip chart up at the front of the room so it keeps us on track with why we are here, so every time you look at the flipchart you are reminded of what you are gaining from the course and can feel good about the fact that you are moving towards it. Now, is this a good time to start talking about... [Good solid anchor of the benefits, firing off the strategy you have been layering in].

[A little later as they are starting to get some content you might suggest a stronger future paced bind]... *Let us go back to the flipchart for a second and I would invite you to notice that you have started to get some of the content you need for these results. So keep coming back to the chart because every time you look at the chart you will notice you have a little more of what you need and can feel even better about looking back from the future towards now and realising this course as the beginning of all these results you have got.* [Often when I have got this totally right the delegates have asked to keep the chart after the course has ended.]

Hypnotic Seduction: An Example of NLP Persuasion

So you are into the conversation, built some rapport and have your subject nicely going into a powerfully erratic state (I know it should be erotic, but you haven't seen my love life), and you are now looking to future pace, amplify and bind that to you...

You... like me probably look back from the future to see the start of the great things in your life [if you are up for it at this point be pointing at your groin... remembering the anchoring].

What I mean is, when you look back on your past to certain events you can realise that this is the start of a great new adventure. [Notice the change in tenses and the ambiguity here am I talking about now, this event, a past event or what?]

This happens to me often, when you do this [switching referential index] *it's funny how much the more you try to let go of the event the more you keep going back to it, getting more and more excited about what you are starting now...* [More do (x) then more (y) happens pattern... a great cause and effect bind].

...starting now with me I meet someone that you just want to spend time with, get to know more closely and just know you are having a great time with [run on sentence, switching referential index, and embedded command galore].

When I do this, you find yourself thinking of that person [pointing to yourself of course] *at odd moments of the day, like every time you step into the shower, or whenever you switch on a light switch* [here is the bind... suggesting that they think of you every time they do a very

```
common  action...  you  sneaky  people...  but  let's
amplify this a little].
```

When I have met someone I really like this feels really good because every time you picture them and realise all the things you like about them you just get that great feeling deep inside and it just gets stronger and stronger every time you take the step or flick the switch.

Now I wouldn't be so presumptuous to suggest that is happening to us now... but wouldn't it be fun if you could look back from the future and see yourself as having this as the start of a great new adventure?

Covert NLP Persuasion For a Networking Event

After you have built some rapport and decided that this person is someone you want to develop more of a relationship with you might say something like this:

I have had a good time speaking with you and I hope you are seeing the benefits of us doing some work together. [The VAdK strategy being layered in right from the start]

[As you hand over your card you might say something like] *I don't know when will be a good time for you to call me. Whether that is next month, next week or even sooner* [notice the time frame getting shorter], *but when the time is right you will see my name on this card, remember the benefits of our discussion today and feel good about phoning* [there is that strategy again].

Anyway, we need to go and network with other people so just keep in mind that we should meet up to discuss some future ventures. Wouldn't it be great if we were to sometime in the future look back to now having completed a couple of successful projects and just feel good about this being the start of that process?

NLP Business Applications: Persuasion Tactics

Getting What You Want From Your Senior Management Using NLP Persuasion Tactics

It is one thing to use NLP techniques to build great programmes and projects that can have a serious impact on results, but often it is key individuals that will either make or break the project. Particularly when dealing with culture change you need all your influential managers working for you. Sometimes this can be a challenge, particularly if they are senior to you.

Below are the edited highlights of an email interchange I have had with an extremely good manager who leads a team and has created some fabulous results. Barry has wanted to take this further but has been having some trouble convincing more senior managers to commit their time, energy and resources. This is how he got their commitment.

NLP Business Tactics: The Results

As this is an ongoing story and some of the people involved would not be pleased if they knew how easily they can be swayed to doing the right thing for the company all the names (including Barry) have been changed. Here is the testimonial I received and below it the strategies I suggested to Barry to create these results:

Thanks Rintu your help is really appreciated.

Things are on the up!

Sharon sent me a note about the presentation with a bit tagged on about what our targets were. (I have given her these previously so the fact she asked I knew she wasn't reading what I was sending!) I suggested we get together to discuss the coaching and targets and how this will improve her centre's results.

I used some of your techniques and got her full agreement that the managers need to do more to manage their teams and that my team is pivotal to increasing results. It was a great meeting so thanks for your help.

I also used the opportunity to involve her in a selection process I was going through for recruiting a new team member. Of course I knew who I wanted but I got her thinking it was her decision.

I also showed her some applications forms I had received that were very poor but had been signed off by one of her senior managers. Again I made her feel it was her that was surprised at the poor quality being recommended and got her to agree we need the best possible people coaching the operational teams.

All in all I am making progress!

Thanks Barry

The NLP techniques and hypnotic patterns that I described to Barry in my email below are a mixture of techniques from two great persuasion artists that anyone serious about this field should read, although approach this from a psychological rather than NLP or hypnosis angle...

NLP Persuasion Resources

The first is a book by Robert Cialdini called *Influence: Science and Practice*. This is required reading for anyone that is interested in how to persuade or influence others. In the patterns I explain below there are several of Cialdini's principles involved.

The second book is by David Lieberman and is called *Get Anyone to Do Anything*. This book approaches persuasion from a traditional psychological perspective and has some great tactics. When you read this book you will see Lieberman's tactics on getting people to return your calls as part of the structure of what I suggested Barry try out on his senior manager.

The parts of the email that I sent Barry with the tactics and patterns I suggested are pasted in below:

Hi Barry

I can sense your frustration and here is a thought... Instead of fighting it, work with it. So if you can get that meeting with Sharon here are a couple of things you can add in to the mix.

The meeting objectives (not necessarily for anyone else's eyes) would be something like:

- Getting Sharon to openly and publicly praise the results your team has got.

- Getting Sharon to buy in (publicly) to the ideas you have for moving this forward.

- Turning around or at least negating the attitude of her senior managers.

Here is structure for the meeting (without content, sorry I'm not that good):

1. Benefit statement of what can be achieved by implementing new ideas.

2. How we got to where we are... including a quick run through of your current presentation.

3. Feedback Sandwich for one of senior managers for supporting the coaching team... I'll explain this bit a little lower down.

4. New ideas coach and facilitate this so she feels like she is creating or contributing to these ideas.

5. Get agreement and seal commitment to the ideas (easy to do if you get point 4 right).

6. Future Pace the benefits again.

Okay, point 3. Let's say for example you are targeting Richard as the senior manager you want to deal with and you want him to release more time from his team managers so you can coach them. A cut down version of the feedback sandwich in your discussion with Sharon would be:

Praising Richard for his support of the work you are doing specifically by... fill in examples (they don't have to be right, just plausible and connected).

The phrase so far is open, public and specific to things that he is doing to completely support the aims and objectives of your coaching team... AND WHAT WOULD MAKE IT EVEN BETTER IS WHEN he... (fill in what you want him to do).

Then to seal it down you tell Sharon it was Richard who gave you the idea in the first place.

Now the statement looks like:

Praise supporting the team by specific behaviours, what will make this even better is when Richard releases his managers on a regular basis to be coached by you.

This was an idea Richard gave you when you had a coffee with him a month ago when he was talking about... fill in any plausible connected conversation you have had with him...

Anyway this works because people are unlikely to turn away open praise... particularly when it is specific and targeted at their behaviour. I have used this sort of pattern to build cult like followings out of managers when I worked in the corporate world. Basically agree with whatever they do, openly praise them for it AND link it to supporting whatever it is you want from them.

Hope it helps

Rintu

NLP Patterns of Persuasion to Manage Authority

As patterns go this works well when having to deal with people in positions of authority over you or you have no direct control over.

By going to their manager with criticisms you risk alienating yourself and creating enemies.

By walking in with open praise for their actions, making them think the good ideas were theirs and then linking all this to actions you want them to take almost guarantees they will work for you.

A Practical Anchoring Example in a Training Context

An anchoring example I wrote for the Essential Skills forum a few years ago really demonstrates how a trainer can install states in to their delegates quickly and easily.

Demonstrating NLP Anchors

I used to work as a training manager for a large company. On one particular day I had the opportunity to demonstrate some anchoring to a new trainer. I got some interesting results and thought I would just share this stuff with you.

Every morning this group of new starts in my company had to sign a sign-in sheet. So just for the demo, I went in, held up this sheet and started talking to the group. I asked them if they were interested in money. Linked the money interest to the sheet (they don't get paid for the day unless they sign the sheet). I then asked them if it was the money or the things they get from having money that was good for them. Once I had them nicely juiced I again (pointing out the sheet) I reminded them that signing the sheet meant more than just the money for them, getting them to access all sorts of ramped up goodness.

It then occurred to me to tell them that effectively at the beginning of the signature they had no money and by the end of their signature they sort of had loads of money for the day. Anyway, to cut a long story to shreds the next morning my trainer catches up with me during a break just to let me know the day had started in a near riot because she had not walked in with the sign in sheet.

She then followed this up by saying several of the delegates went (this is her phrase, not mine) moist just signing their name. By the third day everyone's signature was getting bigger and more elaborate and it was taking longer and longer to get the sheet back. Apparently when they met their team leader for the first time and they were told that they were tracked through their computer logins they suggested that "just for safety" it would be good if they could sign in on a sheet as well. Some people might call me overly manipulative, but I don't think any more fun could be had over a signature and I am sure they enjoyed the experience much more than I.

NLP Techniques To Motivate a Sales Team

An Example of Looking at NLP Persuasion Skills in a More Global Context

Martin Yuille was working as a sales manager in a large call centre operation when he went through his NLP Practitioner Course. One of his primary applications and outcomes for the course was to be able to motivate his sales team to far greater results. From his course Martin applied a variety of NLP techniques and the results were absolutely astounding.

Martin found that his team were taking more calls, converting more sales and were actually having more fun. He took his team from meeting sales targets to exceeding them and on occasion doubling them. In the long run Martin also found that the attrition rate for his team had fallen whilst several team members went for and secured higher-level jobs.

> The sales operation was based on outbound cold calling in a highly competitive industry. The sales agents face a great deal of rejection. The dialler is set on automatic so there is a constant throughput of calls and agents have little or no time to recompose themselves between calls.

As the call centre is an outsourcing operation the parent company is very demanding and is constantly looking for results. My team were constantly under the threat of redundancy with the parent company threatening to take the project in-house if we didn't reach sales targets. Many of the agents considered the dialling lists poor quality and the sales targets unachievable. As with a lot of call centre sales operations the turnover was high.

My intention on going on an NLP practitioner course was to turn this around. Whilst on the course my whole focus was on how I apply this material to my team. I left with lots of really great ideas and was raring to go. I was really taken aback with the results that I got once I'd implemented these ideas.

The following is a précis of all of the ideas that Martin implemented.

NLP Identity, Values and Beliefs

Martin took the whole of his team into a meeting. He got them to build a cohesive identity of an ideal salesperson and the perfect sales team in that context. He then got them to discuss who they were, what was important to them and their beliefs in that context. Martin then spent time reframing and connecting their personal vision with the ideals that they had come up with. The results of this created a much stronger bond between the agents as well as a clearer sense of purpose and a dramatic change in behaviour.

NLP Anchoring to Change Emotions

Martin noticed that several agents, however resourceful before a call would go into an un-resourceful state when they made a call. Initially he took a few agents and anchored them to clicking a pen top for a confident, happy and resourceful state. Several of the agents grew exceptionally attached to those pens. After some thinking Martin took a different tack. He took the agents and anchored that confident happy and resourceful state to a different trigger. He anchored the state to the beep that came through on the headsets to signify a call coming through from the dialler. This meant that as soon as a call came through the agents were in a confident happy and resourceful state.

Hypnotic Language Patterns in Sales

The final element of Martin's work with his team involved scripting the introduction and training them in objection handling. Using NLP language patterns Martin changed the introductions to the call. He introduced a big benefit statement, an anticipation loop closely followed by a presuppositional question. This meant that the sales agents were actually getting further into a lot more calls. Martin also got his team to brainstorm a lot of the common objections and then he fed them NLP hypnotic language patterns to deal with each objection. Using some of the facilitation and training elements that he learnt Martin actually made the agents feel like they came up with the patterns themselves. This meant they had ownership over the issue and several agents started keeping a book of really effective phrases.

The real issue is having an attitude and the methodology that will allow you to come up with the techniques you need for the context that you have. The results happened because Martin had the ability to take what he had learnt and apply them to the situation that he had. A good NLP practitioner course, instead of just giving you lots of techniques, will show you how to apply a methodology that creates results.

In this application we looked at sales but the same techniques would work in many different areas. Imagine a customer service team; all the same elements above could be applied to them. How about a team of hairdressers? You could apply all the same techniques to any customer facing team. In fact consider a board of directors looking to affect a change within their organisation; you could apply all these elements to them and the areas that they might lead. The issue is not the techniques it is all about creating the flexibility of mind and the methodology. You then apply this to your situation and create the techniques to use. Training and developing the attitude and methodology as well as the technique is where good training differs from other courses.

Advanced Persuasion Techniques: Manage Your Boss

Facilitating Commitment Using Advanced Persuasion Skills

I have just received an email from Bob about how he is using *Advanced Persuasion Patterns* to make his work easier. Here is the email (changed to maintain anonymity):

Rintu, Thanks for lesson one I have just got a great result from it. I have been having problems with my manager. I used to work for a boss that was easy going and let you do things your way. But I have recently moved departments and this new manger was driving me mad.

It started to change last night when I listened to the thing about the communication model. I realised if I changed then the relationship would change. Anyway, today, when she came up to check up... sorry... talk to me instead of getting angry and flustered I started talking to her.

The amazing thing is that we opened up a whole series of discussions and I just threw patterns at her all ending with the commitment pattern in the lesson. She agreed to everything I wanted. I think work is going to be fun again.

If you give me any more of these patterns I thing I might try and take over the whole company.

Thanks
Bob

The commitment pattern is a great way of sealing results, particularly with people that have, or think they have authority over you. Using the facilitative version of the pattern is a perfect way of getting a "boss" to give you what you want particularly when they want you to do something. The general form of this would be:

- Listen to their request.

- Reframe it to include what you want.

- Use a conditional close that includes actions from you and your boss to get both.

- Then use a commitment pattern to seal the deal.

Resources & Next Steps

Now You Have Opened The Door Are You Ready To Step Through To The Really Powerful Persuasion Material?

Advanced Persuasion Patterns...

As you have read through this book you will have seen references to my downloadable persuasion skills course: *Advanced Persuasion Patterns*. This course is a mixture of video presentations, audio recordings and written material that is sent to you in bite sized chunks over a period of six months. It takes all this persuasion skills material to a completely new level.

If you have seen a difference in your persuasive ability over the course of reading and implementing the material in this book, imagine those results multiplied a hundred fold and you will be starting to get close to what can be achieved from *Advanced Persuasion Patterns*. You can read about what others are saying about it at the website: *www.thenlpcompany.com/techniques*

Beyond NLP: The Ultimate Practitioner Course

Obviously the best result you can get would be to book on a face to face course. There is an art to finding an effective NLP Trainer. You can find an article to help on the website, and if you have already decided that I am worth booking that course with, feel free to come and chat for an exclusive deal on my Ultimate Practitioner Course: *www.thenlpcompany.com/nlp-training-courses/nlp-practitioner.php*

Rapport, Anchoring & Non Verbal Communication Skills

Learn all these skills in the comfort of your own home and in your own time. These are complex skills and many NLP Trainers are not effective at training them, but worst still have little true understanding of what is actually going on.

Two trainers I highly recommend are Tom Vizzini and Kim Mcfarland from Essential Skills. Have a look at their website and their products. If you can't afford the time and expense of a face to face course then the video products from *Essential Skills* are... well... essential. You can find their products here: *www.essential-skills.com*

NLP Forums

A great place to find more NLP minded people to talk to on line are NLP Forums. You will find many people from the great names and old hands to the complete newbies discussing, debating and developing new ideas on many aspects of NLP on many forums. They are a great place to discuss ideas and practice patterns.

Books About NLP

Learning NLP from books is not always easy. Most have something worth reading in them but it is often a long, painful process to extract that nugget.

There are few books on NLP that I am prepared to recommend. Many are unnecessarily complex, academic, packed full of jargon and don't give you much that is instantly useable.

Much of the early books from Bandler and Grinder are great but are well reviewed and written up over the internet so go and source them for yourself. The following books I recommend for different reasons:

The NLP WorkBook for Dummies by **Romilla Ready**
This is an excellent primer and introduction to NLP

Influence: Science and Practice by **Robert Cialdini**
Anyone that is interested in persuasion skills should read this book not just because it is not an NLP Book but because it is full of the best influence and persuasion ideas on the planet.

Get Anyone To Do Anything by **David Lieberman**
Great amount of hints, tips and ideas. Not an NLP book and much better for it.

Hypnotic Writing: How to Seduce and Persuade Customers with Only Your Words by **Joe Vitale**
Great book to kick start your hypnotic writing skills

An Extra Free Pattern
Advanced Persuasion Patterns

The following is an excerpt from Lesson One of the e-course entitled, *Advanced Persuasion Patterns.* You can get the rest at *www.thenlpcompany.com/advanced-persuasion-skills.php*

QUICK WINS

Over the first few weeks we will be laying down foundations, processes and strategies to build the programme up. Alongside this I want you to have some quick snappy patterns that you can use immediately to get results. We will do this through some simple patterns and through the daily practice.

Next week you will discover how to covertly embed commands in your language and the week after how to open anticipation loops but for today I want to give you a great language pattern for gaining commitment.

This is a really straightforward question.

What do I have to say or do for you to (x)?

Where (x) is whatever you want your subject to do.

The question is really a thought process. So unlike other patterns this one is more about thinking through where you want your subject's mind to go rather than slavishly repeating the pattern.

What it uncovers is the criteria you need to 'close' the person into doing what you want. The option then is for you to either give them what they are asking for or to negotiate on the point.

The other great thing is you can shift the negotiation points to whatever you like. Let me walk you through a few examples to illustrate.

Notice with each of these statements the 'frame' of the negotiation.

Sales

- What product benefit can I demonstrate for you to want to buy today?

- What discount do I have to offer for you to buy today?

- What one thing can I say that will convince you to buy today?

Getting a Date

- Where would we have to go for you to want go out with me?

- What do I have to say or do to get a date with you?

- What one thing do you need to know about me to want a date?

Parenting

- What reward do you need to do your homework now?

- What punishment do I need to threaten you with to do your homework now?

- What one thing do I need to say or do for you to do your homework?

Trainers

- Spend a few moments writing down the benefits you will get from this training course and decide what you are willing to commit to gaining these skills.

- What do you need to do for you to realise you have gained these skills?
- What is the one thing I can say that will make you realise how much you have gained from this programme?

Coaches/Therapists
- What do you need to realise about yourself to let go of your fear of change?
- What can I say that will allow you to see yourself differently?
- What is the one thing we can discuss today that will give you the biggest result?

Now that you have seen a few examples let us discuss some of the finer points of this pattern.

In the front part of the statement you can frame the things you are prepared to negotiate on. For example in a sales environment where you can't offer a discount the second statement would be of no use to you. When you have a customer that is price sensitive and you can offer a discount this statement would be really useful.

The "one thing" phrase I have used as the third example for each context is an extreme version of a frame. The way I have used it in each of the examples above presupposes that there is just "one thing" that is the issue.

The beauty of this pattern is just that if you give them what they ask for they are completely conditioned to give you what you are asking for.

This is a version of the Reciprocation pattern espoused by Robert Cialdini. We will look at some of his material in some depth in later weeks. But in simple terms if I give you something then you are predisposed to give me something in return. How much more power is there in this pattern when you give someone what they ask for? What the commitment pattern does is force people to tell you what they want within your frames and conditionally closes them on what you want in return.

For this pattern to work you really need some rapport, pacing and leading statements at the front end. These are things we will talk in more depth later but for the moment just consider that this pattern is only going to work in an environment where your subject will take the question seriously.

BUT WHAT IF I DON'T LIKE THE ANSWER?

Just review the first pattern from the *Persuasion Skills Black Book*. Redefine what they say and hit them with another commitment pattern. Here are a couple of examples:

A Dating Conversation
- What do I have to say to get a date with you?
- I won't go on a date with you because you are hideously ugly?
- I agree I may seem ugly and the issue is not my looks but how much fun we can have on a date. Where can we go for you to have fun with me?

A Sales Conversation
- What do I have to say for you to want to buy the product today?
- You would have to say that I can have it for free.
- The issue is not about the expense but how much it is costing you not having the product. What do you need from me to realise how much money you are losing by not buying the product?

Coaching/Parenting/Training Conversation

- What do we need to discuss for you to be more confident to do (x)?
- I don't think I will ever be confident enough to do (x).
- I agree, you don't think you will be confident enough yet, and the issue is not about doing (x), but about raising your confidence. So imagine you could become confident enough to do (x), what do we need to discuss for you to move in that direction?

If you have got a few chapters into the *Persuasion Skills Black Book* then you will recognise agreement patterns, the use of 'and', 'but' and 'yet'... If you haven't got that far in the book just stick to the (x) not (y) patterns... they should be obvious.

This Week's Assignments

Do as many of these as are appropriate to you and just focus on the ones that will get you the biggest results. Remember just ten minutes daily.

Based on the Communications Model listen to a few conversations (eavesdrop, interviews and chat shows on TV, listen to the radio). Listen for the assumptions that have to be made for their statement to be true. For example my "one thing" phrases above assume that only "one thing" is the issue. This is a warm up for being able to elicit a personality profile in a matter of minutes that we will start on next week.

Read through the sales letter that brought you here and spot how many times I use the commitment pattern in written form.

Have a think about Cialdini's Reciprocation idea. How have you seen me use it? How could you adapt the idea to work for you?

Write a few commitment patterns and randomly use them on a few people for the practice. Here are a few example patterns but feel free to use any that you come up with:

- "What do I have to do for you to make me a cup of tea?"
- "What can I say to convince you to turn the TV over?"
- "What do you need to think about to make you smile?"

The last one is an example of process based language that we can use to elicit and anchor emotions. Also notice there is no commitment from you in the frame of the question. If you use this particular question just notice how much people will smile automatically as they start to think through the question.

So that's it for this week. Just remember 10 minute chunks and have fun with it. There is a difference between practice and action. If we practice enough you won't realise when you are automatically putting it into action.

Cheers

About Rintu Basu

As an NLP Training Consultant and Coach Rintu Basu specialises in developing people and businesses to maximise their performance in any area. He has developed and trained strategies in many diverse subjects from sales and business development to learning musical instruments and playing winning poker.

Rintu has spent the last fifteen years training hard nosed, practical and often cynical people in communications skills, hypnosis and NLP. Having a pragmatic engineering background as well a broad base of experience in business he has a unique slant on personal development. Rintu has developed a methodology for taking NLP hypnotic language patterns and using them in real world settings to help people get what they want out of life.

As well as running certified NLP courses and maintaining an exclusive coaching practice Rintu is delivering persuasion skills courses based on his individual perspective on the use of hypnotic language patterns.

Learn more at: www.thenlpcompany.com

"This fast-moving, entertaining book is loaded with great ideas you can use immediately to increase your sales."
BRIAN TRACY author of 'The Psychology of Selling'

Act Your Way To Sales Success

SELL YOUR SELF!

BRYAN McCORMACK

Foreword by RINTU BASU author of 'Persuasion Skills Black Book'

www.bookshaker.com

BARE KNUCKLE
NEGOTIATING

KNOCKOUT NEGOTIATION TACTICS THEY WON'T TEACH YOU AT BUSINESS SCHOOL

Download **FREE** 'Bare Knuckle' **Bonuses**

SIMON HAZELDINE
FOREWORD BY DUNCAN BANNATYNE OBE
from BBC TV's "Dragons' Den"

www.bookshaker.com